The Loose Canon

(Complete Second Edition)

By Various Devoted Pastafarians

The Loose Canon (Complete Second Edition)
Copyright © 2014 by Various Devoted Pastafarians

This book was printed after February 5, 2018.

ISBN: 978-0578136660

Proclamations of the Councils of Olive Garden

Second Announcement Regarding Canonical Belief

1 "His Holiness the Flying Spaghetti Monster is Eternal, without beginning and without end, and with a whole tangled mess in the middle.

2 He willed All That There Is into existence when He saw fit to do so and in the order He chose.

3 He prankishly thwarts all human attempts to find out exactly when or how this might have occurred.

4 He has chosen, in His Holy Sauced Wisdom, to reveal only these certain truths: that after the Earth itself, came mountains, trees and a midgit/midget (but not necessarily in that order), and that thereafter He took three days off, Friday being the Holiest among them.

5 What came next is the subject of much great lore passed from the midgit/midgets

down through the ever-dwindling pirate population, also the Holy Inspired Works revealed to and gathered by His Faithful Followers, and attempts at scientific conjecture, each of which have varying levels of accuracy and entertainment value.

6 His Saucy Orbs do look with Delight upon that which is well-written.

7 For as His Noodly Appendages Do Touch Us, so too do they touch even the smallest atoms of the universe, and re-arrange them for His Own Holy Amusement, so as to drive scientists insane.

8 And thus, if Creationism is to be taught as Science, then the Great and Holy Truth of the Creation of the Universe by His Holiness the Flying Spaghetti Monster must also be taught."

-the First Council of Olive Garden

Third Announcement Regarding Canonical Belief

1 These are crappy times for the Church of the Flying Spaghetti Monster.

2 The Dark Lord Darwin roams the world
unchallenged and his Science taints mankind with reason.

3 The Empiricists win more and more court cases against us Creationists and the Scientists add more and more proof to their already flawless theories and facts.

4 It seems the FSM is too drunk and/or lazy to repel this coming enlightenment.

5 But all is not lost and hope still remains.

6 Our numbers continue to grow, nearing 100,000 Pastafarians, this summer has been pretty cool, and now, the first edition of the Loose Canon is finally nearing completion.

7 The Loose Canon is an endeavor our scribes, prophets, captains, and preachers have faithfully worked on since the

ancient days of the Church and soon copies of the psuedofinished work will be available to all Pastafarians to serve as a beacon of hope in these desperate times.

8 I say it will be psuedofinished because the Loose Canon should never be finished.

9 Future holy men and women and robots will unveil more theological ideas and histories and the views of the Church will probably change with time.

10 So in the interest of being a perpetually modern religion, Councils of Olive Garden must periodically convene to compile new editions of the Loose Canon.

11 In my opinion, the texts of the Canon should never be altered or eliminated, however, any text, no matter how contradictory, can be canonized.

12 Even this first edition has texts that contradict each other and even the Gospel of the FSM.

13 This fits with the philosophy of our Church.

14 One should not have blind faith in a holy text.

15 One should not take a holy text as word for word truth.

16 After all, it's just a book written by imperfect humans, not by the all-knowing Flying Spaghetti Monster.

17 Though I could be completely wrong about all of this.

18 Future Pastafarians are just gonna have to think for themselves and make up their own minds.

19 So with that said, I hope the congregation will enjoy the Loose Canon.

20 I hope everyone gets a laugh out of its stories and ponders the wisdom of its teachings.

21 So stay tuned maties cause it's coming and it'll be awesome when it does.

22 And maybe that dick, Darwin, will think twice about tempting us with his evidence and facts when he sees how

psyched we are about our newly made book filled with revelations from the Flying Spaghetti Monster.
 23 RAmen,

- The Second Council of Olive Garden

The Book of Ruthie

Chapter 1

1 Now it came to pass in the days when the captains ruled, that there was a shortage of Spanish galleons to raid.

2 And a certain pirate of Bethlehem went to sojourn in the country of England, he and daughter.

3 And the name of the pirate was Elimelech (Hebrew for 'Pasta with cream sauce), and the name of his daughter was Naomi.

4 And they came into the country of England, and continued there.

5 But the English were big fans of the Dark Lord Darwin.

6 And Elimelech, Naomi's father, was strung up for piracy and she was left alone to hide from the King's men.

Chapter 2

1 And she met a Christian woman, Ruthie, and it was love at first sight.

2 After several dates, Naomi said unto Ruthie, "I am the daughter of a pirate, and if you associate with me the English will hang you along with me. So go, and save yourself."

3 But Ruth embraced her, saying, "Do not press me to leave you or to turn back from following you! Where you go, I will go;
where you lodge, I will lodge; your people (pirates) shall be my people (pirates),
and your god my god (as it is cool if you are both Christian and Pastafarian).

4 Where you die, I will die—there I will be buried. May the FSM do thus and so to me,
and more as well, if even death parts me from you!"

5 When Naomi saw that she was determined to go with her, she said no more to her.

6 But still not wanting to dance the hempen jig, they went back to live together in Bethlehem.

Chapter 3

1 Years passed, and one day, Ruthie came home from a day's work of plundering and she greeted Naomi.

2 And Naomi said unto her, "Call me not Naomi, call me Pissed Off, for our Lord Glob has dealt bitterly with me."

3 "Why? What happened?" asked Ruthie.

4 "Some people were making fun of us for being gay. And the FSM did nothing to stop their criticism yet again."

5 And there was thunder and whirling wind, and the FSM did descend from Heaven.

6 "My ears are burning.

7 Really, I overcooked myself.

8 I know, I know, bad joke.

9 Anyway...

10 Heathens!" He boomed, "Gays shall burn on the great stove of Hell for all eternity!"

11 He paused, "Nah, I'm just messing with you.

12 We don't even have a Hell, much less a great stove.

13 But really, you're not hurting anyone.
14 You can live your life however the hell you want."
15 "That's what we tell people," said Ruthie, "But we are still condemned."
16 "Seriously?" inquired the FSM, somewhat puzzled, "If I didn't want you to be gay I would've made you straight.
17 Der."
18 "I know, but they say homosexuality is a choice," Naomi added.
19 "Shit, even that argument doesn't work.
20 I'm totally omnipotent; therefore anything you do is the result of my will.
21 So it is still because of me that you're gay.
22 For the record, marriage is the sacred union between a person and person(s)."
23 "I dunno, they're kinda dumb," replied Ruthie.
24 "Chillax.
25 It'll all work out in time.
26 And for now, just ignore the stupid ones.

27 They're stupid," the FSM said compassionately (cause He's freaking God, and He's supposed to be compassionate).

28 And Ruthie and Naomi walked away as the camera panned out. "You know 'Naomi' is 'I moan' spelled backwards?" Ruthie said.

29 "You totally stole that from Waiting...," Naomi replied.

30 And they lived happily ever after.

Please attend the Pastafarian Convention on August 9, 2024 at Best Western Plus Bradenton Gateway Hotel 2215 Cortez Road W, Bradenton, FL 34207

https://www.facebook.com/PastafarianLooseCanon/

The Torahtellini Part 1

Chapter 1 – A Contradictory Account of the Genesis

1 In the beginning, the Flying Spaghetti Monster made some stuff in like a week or something.

2 He was drunk a good deal of the time, so the whole account is a little sketchy.

3 But at some point He made a midgit out of dirt.

4 And it all was pretty sweet.

5 The FSM then planted the Olive Garden of Eden, where He put the midgit that He had made.

6 Then in His infinite wisdom, He planted the Pine Tree of Knowledge of Good and Evil, which served absolutely no purpose.

7 And the Lord Glob commanded the midgit, saying, "Of every tree in the garden you may eat freely, except for the Pine Tree of Knowledge of Good and Evil.

8 You shall not eat of it, for in the day that you do eat from it, you shall surely die. DIE. Scary right?"

9 And the FSM didn't want Midgit to be lonely, so He made dinosaurs and such to keep him company.

10 But Midgit wasn't a big fan of the dinosaurs, as Velociraptors eat things, and he was a thing that was bite sized.

11 So the FSM made from the dirt an equal creature, a lady midgit, and brought her unto Midgit.

12 And the lady midgit said, "Because I am a midgit and a lady, I am named Lady Midgit."

13 And they were both bare-assed, and they were not ashamed.

14 Now the snake was one of the craftiest of all of the FSM's creatures.

15 And the snake said unto Lady Midgit and Midgit, "The pine nuts from the Pine Tree of Knowledge of Good and Evil are pretty delicious.

16 Also, if you eat them, you will no longer be idiots, and will know right from wrong, which is nice too.

17 You guys should try them."

18 "No, we cannot. The Pine Tree of Knowledge of Good and Evil is off-limits and eating its nuts will kill us," they said.

19 "Don't worry about it," the snake replied,

20 "First, you won't die.

21 The whole creation thing has gone to the FSM's head and He's been overly dramatic lately.

22 Second, there's really no good reason for him to deny the pine nuts from the Pine Tree of Knowledge of Good and Evil from you.

23 Again, He's just being an idiot."

24 And so the couple ate pine nuts from the Pine Tree of Knowledge of Good and Evil and indeed, they were delicious.

25 And they were no longer idiots and now had morality.

26 They saw that they were naked and became embarrassed.

27 So they made leaves into hats to wear.

28 And the FSM wanted to go to the bar and went looking for the midgit couple so they could buy Him a beer.

29 When He came upon them, He saw that they had become aware of their nakedness and became angry,

30 "Hats! You know you're naked!?

31 You ate my nuts (yeah, lame joke), didn't you?!"

32 "The snake pointed out that You had no good reason to not let us eat the pine nuts," they said meekly.

33 "Grrrrrr," growled the FSM, but then he paused, "Oh, well I guess I really don't have a good reason...

34 and I guess it would be unbelievably dumb to give you free will but not morality.

35 And because you have shown me the error of my ways," He said to the snake, "I shall make you a divine creature.

36 And from now on, you shall resemble My noodly appendage,"

37 He turned to the midgits, "And you two midgits, you don't have to stay here in the Garden just so I have people to kiss my ass.

38 I shall bestow upon you puny mortals independence.

39 So go forth, be fruitful and multiply. That means have sex."

Chapter 2 – The Dawn of Evil

1 And Midgit "knew" Lady Midgit and she conceived and bore a son, Cain.

2 After a second "knowing", Lady Midgit bore another son, Abel.

3 Their parents raised them to be good Pastafarians.

4 Abel had great respect for his noodly Lord and would always offer the FSM finely cooked fettuccine alfredo and baked ziti.

5 But Cain, lazier and kind of a douche, offered only cheap macaroni and cheese.

6 And one time, the FSM, drunk and hungry, said unto Cain, "What gives puny mortal?

7 Thou shall be more like your brother, and give me good food.

8 For I am your god and ye shall kiss My ass."

9 Cain replied, "Bite me."

10 And in a drunken rage, the FSM banished Cain to Antarctica.

11 He cursed Cain, and turned him into a penguin, the unholiest of creatures (See the Gospel of the Flying Spaghetti Monster).

12 Cain, outraged at the FSM, decided to get even by making new being, Frostenstein the Snowdemon, an evil monster bent on opposing the FSM and destroying the midgitkind.

13 In a grotesque parody of the FSM's noodly appendages, Frostenstein is covered in icicles.

14 They are cold and tasteless.

15 Instead of their touch helping people, they pierce and chill.

16 Frostenstein and Cain devised a vile teaching that goes against all the FSM is about, Science.

17 Between the Science, VD incrusted fallen strippers, and army of demented snowman, Frostenstein strikes down all the midgits he can find.

18 But the FSM, who had sobered up for a couple minutes, went back to Cain, apologized, and unpenguinified him.

19 But Cain was worried about Frostenstein, the evil menace he created.

20 And the FSM said that it was cool, since He could use a good opponent to keep Him on His toes and solves a big freaking dilemma, since the FSM is all good, can't create evil Himself.

21 And so, for thousands of years, the FSM and Frostenstein would battle.

22 But Frostenstein, being made out snow and ice, had a limited range and could only kill people in the winter.

23 So he decided to play FSM and genetically engineered himself into a scary sea monster, the Kraken.

24 Keeping with the mockery of the noodly appendages, he grew slimey and difficult to chew tentacles.

25 For a few hundred years, he swam the seas, eating all the pirates in his path.

26 The pirates dwindled, but a renewed force would emerge in the Golden Age of Piracy, the Buccaneers, a combined force of all four Pirate Fleets (more on that later) who would challenge the Kraken for supremacy of the sea.

27 So the Kraken again changed form.

28 The demon became Davy Jones, a tentacle faced creature and not only a caricature of the FSM, but of mankind as well.

29 He formed his own dark realm in the ocean depths, the Locker.

30 There he forced those he corrupted with constant schooling and boring education.

31 The pious pirates who would not convert faced his phantom ship's cannons or his rusty cutlass blade.

32 But Davy Jones' form was intimidating and it was hard to have serious talks with men in order to corrupt them.

33 He found a young man, studying to be a holy captain in an English tavern.

34 This man, Charles Darwin, was wealthy and had a lot of connections and therefore influential among men.

35 Davy Jones struck Darwin down and assumed his identity.

36 He formed his most insulting satire of His noodly appendages yet, a gray, itchy beard that wasn't nearly as appetizing as pasta.

37 The new Darwin was the most powerful incarnation of evil ever.

38 He used his influence to corrupt mankind with his new trick, the Deception of Evolution.

39 But worse, he convinced the ninjas, longtime enemies of the pirates, to begin a great purge of the pirate race (See Darwin's Purge).

Chapter 3–The Great Accidental Smiting of Almost All of Mankind

1 And Abel begat Enos, who begat Cainan, who begat Mahalaleel, who begat Jared, who begat Enoch, who begat Methuselah, who begat Lamech, who begat Noah.
2 And Noah was five hundred years old and Noah begat Ham, Cheese, and Omel.
3 One day, the FSM was drunk and hungry and decided to cook some pasta.
4 But in His inebriated clumsiness, He spilled the sauce.
5 Meanwhile, down on Earth, Noah saw a cascade of spaghetti sauce pouring down from the heavens and rolling over the desert.
6 "Jesus Christ!" he shouted,
7 "Everybody get on the boat!"
8 Noah, a typical lazy Pastafarian, did not
build said boat, but bought it, for a pretty good price actually.

9 So Noah and his family were saved, simply by accident, while the rest of mankind was washed away by the flood of
spaghetti sauce, also by accident, but an epically much crappier accident.

10 The FSM, seeing what He had done, hurried down to Earth to help, but still being drunk, only grabbed non-human animals from the red waves.

11 Also, being lazy, He stacked all the animals on Noah's boat, saying, "Don't worry puny mortal, I'll give you credit."

12 And the FSM stumbled back up to heaven to watch some TV and pass out.

13 Over a month later, Noah and his family, having eaten most of the dinosaurs and knee deep in animal poo, were still floating on the global sea of sauce.

14 On the fortieth day, the FSM was drunk and hungry, and seeing all that sauce on

Earth, His eyes lit up and He went down and sopped it all up with some good Italian bread.

15 He saw Noah's family, the last humans, and the countless dead bodies.

16 "Oops," He said.

17 "Dick," said Noah.

Chapter 4 –Pirate Fleets Descend from Noah

1 This is the account of the descendents of Noah's sons, Ham, Cheese, and Omel; children were born to them after the Flood.

2 The sons would spread across the Earth on the backs of dinosaurs and people the world

3 (except for the Native Americans, Africans, and Australian Aborigines who I guess came from some other god capable of creating humans).

4 Omel stayed on the coast of the Mediterranean, mostly because his Ankylosaurus was so damn slow.

5 He begat many sons, one, Nimrod, went unto Israel and begat some more sons leading to Abraham, who begat Ishmael and Isaac.

6 Ishmael would go unto the Far East (bringing the idea of pasta with him) and start a great pirate clan there, the Wokou.

7 Some prophets, Lao Tzu, Chuang Tzu, and Confucius would be of the Wokou Fleet.

8 Mongols, who did not eat the divine meal of pasta, but only horse blood (for reals) and so had not been touched by His noodly appendage.

9 These conquerors would spread east, battling the Wokou.

10 The Eastern Pastafarians, in their time of trouble, would build a monument to the FSM in the image of His noodly appendage, in an attempt to gain His favor.

11 The FSM wasn't paying any attention, but thankful, the monument acted as a great wall, and held off the Mongols.

12 Isaac would buy a summer home in Italy as it's so damn hot in Israel come summertime.

13 His descendents would form another great pirate group, the Corsairs.

14 Some prophets, Pirate Mosey, Captain Dave, and the Great Pirate Solomon would be of the Corsair Fleet.

15 But the descendents of Omel, with the exception of Abraham's lineage, would become corrupt and turn away from the FSM, plagiarizing His teachings, worshipping heathen gods, and harboring ninjas.

16 This would lead to the great Pirato-Ninja Wars, and for generations, the pious Corsair captains would battle the ninja threat on the Mediterranean.

17 Cheese went unto India on a pterodactyl (which the FSM doth proclaim to be a dinosaur to piss off the smart-ass paleontologists).

18 His descendents, another pirate Fleet, the Samudra-dasyu, would spread north in to Central Asia, and as far east as Iran;

19 their Fleet would sail the Indian Ocean and their gurus were among the best Pastafarian theologians.

20 Some prophets, Ramanuja, Cārvāka, and Kamsa would be of the Samudra-dasyu Fleet.

21 But ninjas disguised as holy men, going by the name of Hari Krishnas (kṛṣṇa being a Pastafarian demigod), would bring war to India and decimate the Samudra-dasyu's numbers.

22 Ham would go unto Scandanavia on a Triceratops.

23 His descendents would favor cod to spaghetti, which distanced them from the FSM.

24 The resulted in an increase in their height, which they noticed and realized the error in their ways.

25 They formed the Society for Piratical Renewal aka the Vikings, the fourth Pirate Fleet.

26 They would eventually move south forming the Germanic and Celtic civilizations.

27 The great Pastafarian priests of the Celts, the Druids, were renowned for their theology.

28 Some prophets, Bobby Henderson, Ushnor, and Ulf Hamson would be of the Viking Fleet.

29 The corrupt Omelite tribe, the Romans, would invade and kill off most of the Celts, and the Germans invaded in retaliation, beating the Romans, but losing many of their pirates in the process.

30 The Four Fleets, crippled by ninjas, Mongols, Hari Krishnas, and Romans, and the Kraken, would see a reprieve, and at
the peak of the Golden Age of Piracy, would merge into a new Pirate Fleet, the Buccaneers.

31 Some prophets, Long John Silver, the Sea-Cook, Captain Jack Sparrow, and

Black Bob would be of the Buccaneer Fleet.

32 These devout and pious pirates would sail across the seven seas, spreading His word and doing good deeds.

Chapter 5 –The Ivory Tower of Babel

1 Now the whole Earth had one religion, one single train of thought dominated by the FSM.

2 And the puny mortals said to one another, "Come, let us think for ourselves.

3 Let us figure out how the world works and not just take the FSM's word for it.

4 You know how much of a drunk He is."

5 And they built a great university, the Ivory Tower of Babel, and began solving the mysteries of the universe.

6 Then the FSM came down to the Tower, which the puny mortals had built.

7 And the FSM said, "Look, they are one people, and they have one great academy;

and this is only the beginning of what they will do; nothing that they propose to do will be impossible for them.

8 That's nice...

9 Oh shit! My illusion!

10 They're gonna figure out that the world isn't nearly as old as I made it look.

11 Come, let us go down, and confuse their academics, so that it is split into many fields: philosophy, science, theology, art, and mathematics.

12 And so they will constantly argue over whose field is better, and they will never
accomplish anything."

13 And the FSM did that.

Chapter 6 –The Humbling of the Lord Glob

1 These are the descendents of Nimrod: some guys begat more guys who begat another guy who begat Abraham.

2 And the FSM decided it was time to finally get the whole pirate thing rolling.

3 He decided in His infinite wisdom that this random guy, Abraham, would be the first pirate.

4 And the FSM came unto Abraham.

5 "Abraham!" boomed the FSM overdramatically, "I am your Lord Glob, the creator of the world and God of the first midgit and tree!"

6 Abraham looked up, "Hey."

7 The FSM was a little confused, "You're not impressed?

8 You're supposed to be in awe and bow or something."

9 "Meh," said Abraham,

10 "Whatevs dude."

11 "Oh, hmm, well anyway, I've decided to make your descendents great pirates who will sail the seven seas and stuff."

12 "That's pretty cool.

13 But there's a problem; I'm impotent."

14 "No worries," said the FSM,

15 "I'm totally omnipotent, I'll take care of it.

16 So, some of my heavenly strippers just got back from Sodom and Gomorra and they tell me there's all kinds of freaky sex there.

17 So let's head over there, get smashed, and try out your new virility."

18 "Haha, ok dude."

19 And they went unto a seedy bar in Sodom, and later, drunkenly stumbled over to a strip joint in Gomorra.

20 The FSM and Abraham got laid and there was much rejoicing.

21 The next morning, a hooker was pregnant with Abraham's son and the FSM had the clap.

22 And the FSM was displeased, as He hates getting gonorrhea.

23 "Roar!" roared the FSM,

24 "That damn lady gave me gonorrhea!

25 I hate getting gonorrhea!

26 I will smite everyone in those cities for this!"

27 "Dude," said Abraham,

28 "Screw that.

29 First, not everyone there gave you crabs.

30 Second, you should've been smart and worn a condom.

31 Third, you're a god; you should be more responsible than that.

32 Like seriously dude, have you read the last five chapters?

33 You're a total douche.

34 If you want people to like you and worship you, you need to be much cooler."

35 "Wow dude, You're [sic] right," the FSM said meekly,

36 "I gotta get my act together.

37 You're a good friend for not fearing me and being honest with me.

38 We're like totally biffles, so no more formalities, I will call you Abe.

39 And from now on, I will make it clear to my people that I am imperfect.

40 No more ego, no more self-centeredness.

41 I will request that my followers critique me and call me on any errors or misdeeds.

42 I will also request that they must not rely solely on me for help.

43 I will put in an effort, but jackass that I am, they should focus on helping each other.

44 These are the two greatest of my suggestions."

45 "Sweet," said Abe.

46 "Heck yes," said the FSM,

47 "Come, let us celebrate and go get smashed."

The Torahtellini Part 2

Chapter 1

1 It is written, back in the ancient days, the Flying Spaghetti Monster enjoyed drinking with his human buddy, Abe.

2 One night, Abe told the FSM he had to get up early in the morning and couldn't hang out with Him all night.

3 The FSM, who had had a few too many beers, was depressed and weepy.

4 He said to Abe, "You're such a douche.

5 What am I supposed to do the rest of the night?"

6 "Dude, we'll chill tomorrow.

7 It's no biggie," said Abe.

8 "No dude, it's not just this.

9 You've really been a crappy friend lately."

10 "Well I got a family now.

11 I got responsibilities.

12 I can't always screw around and drink with you all the time."

13 "Screw that man.

14 I'm your god.

15 You need to prove your loyalty to me."

16 "Ok, that's fair.

17 What do you want me to do?"

18 "Kill your son."

19 "No way man.

20 I can't."

21 "Do it."

22 "Dude, it's..."

23 "Do it," the FSM interrupted.

24 "Really?"

25 "Yeah dude, you gotta listen to me.

26 I'm your god."

27 "Alright," Abe said sheepishly.

28 "Ahhhh, you got punk'd!

29 I wouldn't make you do that.

30 Aww, you shoulda seen your face when I said that."

31 "Yeah..."

32 "Instead, you gotta chop off the tip of your dick."

33 Abe laughed, "You're not getting me this time."

34 The FSM giggled and took a drink.

35 "Nope, totally cereal.

36 It's like the 5th Commandment: Thy Noodle shall not be bigger than Mine."

37 "But we don't have Commandments," Abe protested.

38 "Shh."

39 "Ok, fine."

40 And so Abe circumcised himself (yeah, he did it himself).

41 The next day, after miraculously curing His hangover, the FSM remembered the shit He pulled the night before and gave Abe a call.

42 "Hey dude, sorry about the shit I pulled last night."

43 "It's cool," Abe said, "You were pretty wasted."

44 "Yeah, well to make up for it, I decided to give you and your descendents your own land."

45 "Aww sweet dude.

46 I've actually had my eye on Canaan."

47 "No dude, there's already people living there.

48 What would you do, kill them all?"

49 "Uh..."

50 "No, your Promised Land will be the sea.

51 And you get the whole thing, but only on the condition that you and your descendents are pirates.

52 I like pirates.

53 Cool?

54 "Yeah man, it's a deal."

55 And so the Pastament was made.

Chapter 2

1 Generations later, due to a series of mishaps, Abe's descendents had not yet made it to the Promised Land...

2 Pirate Mosey had just finished telling his pirate crew about the eight "I'd Really Rather You Didn'ts" (*see The Gospel of the Flying Spaghetti Monster*).

3 The FSM had another word with Mosey, which was pretty sweet (*see the Book of Piraticus*).

4 They finally left Mount Salsa and continued their journey to the Promised Land.

5 They milled around for years trying to find the sea.

6 Mosey tried convincing them that if they just walked in a straight line, they'd eventually hit the shore.

7 But his crew would frequently grow impatient and insist that they make turns here and there and they just wound up constantly going around in big circles.

8 When the Quartermaster decided they should make a left at Jericho, Mosey got fed up and finally put his foot down.

9 "Guys, quit being back seat wanderers!

10 We're walking straight from now on!"

11 "Captain," said the First Mate, "Sorry, but this is really getting aggravating.

12 Maybe if we just had a beer or two..."

13 And so the FSM, taking pity on His followers, provided them with a keg and told Mosey to tap it.

14 But Mosey, still frustrated, hacked it with his cutlass.

15 Beer splattered everywhere, getting the pirates sticky and spilling all out onto the ground.

16 "Dude!" the FSM shouted from Heaven,

17 "What the hell?

18 I try to do something nice for my people and you go and ruin it.

19 Just for that, you're not allowed in the Promised Land."

Chapter 3

1 But Pirate Mosey remained cool and continued to fulfill his responsibility to his people.

2 He prepared for their entrance into the Promised Land and trained his crew on various piratical methods.

3 He gave his officers greater responsibilities in order to get them ready for commanding crews on the sea.

4 He appointed the most devout of the men, the boatswain Josh, to be the future Commodore of the Pirate Fleet.

5 When they finally came within sight of the ocean, Mosey sent look-outs up onto a hill to see if they should approach.

6 But a storm was on the horizon, and the water was full of sea monsters.

7 They decided to head back into the wilderness for a while.

8 Unfortunately they got lost again, and they wandered around in the desert for forty years before they got back to the shore.

9 The FSM came to them and instructed them that they should build many ships and split the men along family lines into 12 crews.

10 He then turned to Mosey and said, "Hey dude, I was a little hungover and grumpy the day I said you weren't allowed in the Promised Land.

11 If you wanna go too, it's cool."

12 "No, your Noodliness," said Mosey, "I messed up.

13 It's only right that I stay behind.

14 But I would like to renew the Pastament.

15 We have remained loyal and become pirates like you wanted.

16 Will you allow us to live on the Promised Land forever?"

17 "Sure," said the FSM.

18 "Sweet," said Mosey.

19 The crews prepared to set sail into the Promised Land, and Pirate Mosey said good bye and gave them one last suggestion,

20 "Hear O Pirates, the Flying Spaghetti Monster is our god, the Flying Spaghetti Monster is yum."

21 And the pirate fleet under Commodore Josh went forth into the sea and established a great dynasty of buccaneers.

The Tale of Dave and Kyodai

Chapter1

1 Now the ninjas gathered their forces for war and assembled at the port of Tortuga.
2 They scattered their men around the local tavern, so that they could ambush the pirates when they came ashore.
3 Soon after, Captain "Dead Sole" Paulson and his pirate crew sailed into port.
4 They eagerly went to the tavern, thirsty for rum.
5 The ninjas sprung forth and attacked the pirates.
6 The pirates, though peaceful, were forced to fight for their lives.
7 A champion named Kyodai, who was from Osaka, came out of the ninja horde.
8 He was six cubits and a span tall, as he was unholy and was never touched by His noodly appendage.
9 He was wrapped with his black ninja cloak.

10 In his hand, he held a long sword, dripping with pirate blood.

11 Kyodai stood and shouted to the pirate crew, "Why do you come out and line up for battle?

12 Am I not a ninja, and are you not Dead Sole Paulson's crew?

13 Choose a pirate and have him come down to me.

14 If he is able to fight and kill me, we will become your subjects; but if I overcome him and kill him, you will become our subjects and serve us."

15 Then the ninja said, "This day I defy the ranks of pirates!

16 Give me a man and let us fight each other." On hearing the ninja's words, Dead Sole Paulson and all the pirates were dismayed and terrified.

Chapter 2

1 Now Dave was the son of an Englishman named Jesse, who was from Bath in Somerset.

2 Jesse had eight sons, and in Dead Sole Paulson's time, he was old and well advanced in his years.

3 Jesse's three oldest sons had joined Dead Sole Paulson's crew to man the cannons and plunder trade ships, but Dave was hired as a cabin boy, left to cook for the rest of the crew.

4 After the crew had went ashore at Tortuga, Dave, left behind cause he was underaged, was finally able to make a meal for himself.

5 As he was sitting down to eat a hearty plate of spaghetti and meatballs, he heard swords clashing, muskets firing, and angry "Arrr's" off in the distance.

6 Dave, eager to help his fellow pirates got ready to leave, but remembered his pasta.

7 He was still hungry, so he wrapped up the spaghetti and took it with him as he set out to find the battle.

Chapter 3

1 After wandering around looking for the battle for an hour or two, he finally reached the group of pirates.

2 Dave could see that the pirates and ninjas had separated standing facing each other, with Kyodai standing in between waiting for someone to fight him.

3 Dave ran to greet his fellow crewmates.

4 They told him all about Kyodai and his challenge.

5 Dave asked what'd they plan on doing about him.

6 When Eric, Dave's oldest brother, heard him speaking with the men, he got ticked off and asked, "What the hell are you doing here?

7 Who's cooking our dinner?

8 I know how conceited you are and how wicked your heart is; you came over just to watch the battle, you dildo."

9 "Dude, you didn't even let me tell my side of the story before you started

whining about my evil heart and shit," said Dave.

10 Dead Sole Paulson heard the commotion and came over.

11 Dave said to him, "Don't worry about this ninja, I can take him."

12 Dead Sole Paulson replied, "You can't fight him, you're just a kid and he's badass."

13 But Dave said to the Captain, "I've watched over the food in the galley.

14 Whenever a rat or seagull tried to eat some, I smacked it and when it turned on me, I killed it.

15 I have killed both the rat and the seagull, and this ninja will be like one of them, because he has killed the people of the FSM.

16 The FSM who delivered me from the paw of the rat and the talons of the seagull will deliver me from the hand of the ninja."

17 Captain Dead Sole Paulson said to Dave, "Go and the FSM be with you."

Chapter 4

1 Dave was given a cutlass, a musket, six pistols, a blunderbuss, and a cutlass.

2 Dave said, "I can't use all of this.

3 It's way too much and I've never swung a sword or shot a gun before.

4 I'll probably end up hurting myself more than the ninja."

5 He dropped all the weapons and took from his bag a few long strands of spaghetti and a few meatballs.

6 He folded the spaghetti over a meatball and approached the ninja.

7 Meanwhile, the ninja got ready and walked towards Dave.

8 When he saw Dave was just a kid he got pissed at him.

9 He said to Dave, "I'm gonna mess you up you little punk."

10 Dave said to the ninja, "You come against me with your fancy sword, but I come against you in the name of the FSM,

the God of the pirates, whom you have deified.

11 Today the FSM will hand you over to me, and I'll strike you down and kick you in the nuts.

12 So, I'm gonna mess you up.

13 The ninja approached to fight, and Dave ran to meet him.

14 Dave whipped around the spaghetti and slung the meatball at the ninja, shooting it right down his windpipe.

15 Choking, the ninja fell to the ground.

16 So Dave triumphed over the ninja with spaghetti and meatballs.

17 Without a cutlass in his hand he struck down the ninja.

18 Dave then ran over and kicked Kyodai square in the nuts.

19 Kyodai grunted in discomfort, popping the meatball from his throat.

20 When the other ninjas saw their hero was down and clutching his groin, they turned and ran.

21 The pirates chased them and made sure they left the town.

22 Victorious, they went into the tavern to partake in some well-deserved rum.

23 Proud of the cabin boy, Captain Dead Sole Paulson bought Dave a drink.

24 And there was much rejoicing.

Darwin's Purge

Chapter 1

1 Decades had passed since the Golden Age of Piracy.

2 Pirates had grown arrogant with the knowledge that they were the Flying Spaghetti Monster's chosen people.

3 No longer did they bury treasure to keep it from corrupting others with greed, instead keeping the gold and jewels for themselves.

4 They no longer sailed around distributing candy to young children.

5 They forced their religion on others, demanding that nonbelievers follow the FSM.

6 The great pirate leaders, Pirate Mosey with his divine favor, Captain Dave with his prowess in battle, and the Great Pirate Solomon with his profound wisdom, had moved on to the Beer Volcano and Stripper Factories of Heaven.

7 There was no one left to alter the pirates' sinful course.

8 The Flying Spaghetti Monster would defend them no longer.

Chapter 2

1 A ninja stealthily crept towards his prey.

2 He prepared to leap at the unsuspecting man, but he sensed something was wrong.

3 He turned around to see a bearded old man.

4 He struggled to recognize him in the darkness, but then it came to him; it was the sly demon, the Dark Lord Darwin himself!

5 The ninja pointed his sword at the creature, prepared to defend himself.

6 "Get back fiend!" he shouted, "Or I shall cut you down."

7 "Your skills are no match for me," Darwin said,

8 "I have powers beyond your imagination.

9 You are a ninja, are you not supposed to be stealthy and undetectable?

10 How then did I see you?"

11 Shaken by his apparent lack of sneakiness, the ninja responded, "How?"

12 "I used the dark power of observation.

13 I merely opened my eyes and looked around," Darwin gloated.

14 "Incredible," said the ninja, "Teach me more."

15 "There are four dark powers of Science.

16 I will teach you the other three, but only on the condition that you lead the ninjas in a final purge of the pirates."

17 "I know the pirates and us have fought in the past, but extermination seems like a little too much."

18 "I guarantee, once you learn of the powers, you will want to destroy them all.

19 Do we have a deal?"

20 The ninja thought for a minute.

21 "Yes, it's a deal," he agreed reluctantly.

22 Darwin smiled.

23 "The second power is reason.

24 Use logic in your strategies against the pirates.

25 For example, pirates love to drink rum,
so maybe ambush them at a tavern.

26 Now, this is useful, but don't solely rely on it.

27 Just because something makes sense doesn't mean it's true.

28 So reason must be used with the third power, experimentation.

29 If you do attack the pirates at a tavern and you lose, then try something else.

30 A combination of logic and trial and error, reason and experimentation, will give you an effective method in fighting the pirates."

31 "I see," said the ninja,

32 "These powers do seem powerful, but I still don't feel like killing every last pirate."

33 "That's where the last power comes in.

34 The dark power of evidence.

35 Pirates are always armed with cutlasses and flintlocks; they travel in ships loaded with cannons.

36 They have constantly fought with the ninjas.

37 They are a threat to you and your people.

38 What choice do you have other than to destroy them all?"

39 "Yes!

40 You're right."

41 "I'm a scientist.

42 I'm always right.

43 Now I'm currently working on a deception, the Theory of Evolution, that will destroy the faith of the pirates and prevent them from gaining new converts.

44 It will even hurt the FSM himself, as he put a lot of effort into making the universe appear older than it really is.

45 Evolution will provide an alternative to his practical joke, thus ruining his fun.

46 All the ninjas must do is eliminate the pirates and Pastafarianism will fall.

47 The ninja, jazzed by this information, went forth and spread his new knowledge of Science.

Chapter 3

1 Pirates have never been the most skillful fighters.

2 They are peaceful men and had mostly held off attempted purges by the ninjas in the past by divine intervention from the FSM.

3 But now the FSM had forsaken them for their digressions.

4 Furthermore, they had grown fat and pathetic, perpetually drinking rum and boning wenches, and were in no shape for battling ninjas.

5 This combined with the ninjas mastery of the dark powers of Science meant the pirates didn't stand a chance against the coming doom.

6 The ninjas spread across the land, slaughtering every pirate they found.

7 They hunted them down like bilge rats.

8 Most cowardly fled out into the sea or drowned their sorrows in rum, waiting for the end.

9 Many complained to the FSM and turned against Him for letting this misfortune befall them.

10 But some took a stand and proudly fought to the end, knowing that they had brought this upon themselves.

11 Others repented and prayed to the FSM to apologize for their wrongdoings.

12 The FSM saw these devout pirates and felt bad for condemning his entire following for the sleaze of some.

Chapter 4

1 Captain Black Bob had made it back to his ship after a narrow victory over a ninja assault party.

2 He had lost many of his crew and was feeling depressed.

3 He prayed, "Oh tasty Flying Spaghetti Monster, I realize this destruction must be our fault, but I need to know, what have we done wrong?"

4 "Pirates have become corrupt and have strayed from Pastafarianism.

5 Now I'm not the kinda god to smite those who don't listen to me, but I don't have to protect you either," answered the FSM. "That still sounds pretty lame."

6 "I know, but I'm a god. I got responsibilities and shit.

7 Do you really wanna worship a god who helps out assholes?"

8 "No."

9 "Yeah, well you guys were assholes."

10 "True, but I have repented.

11 I have admitted that I have done wrong."

12 "You doing better than most of your brethren, but you're still not good enough.

13 For example, stop killing ninjas.

14 Remember the second suggestion "Thou ought not do stuff thou already

knowest is wrong, like killing, lying, cheating,
stealing, etc. Dost thou really need these carved into a rock?"

15 Yeah, they may kill you, but at least you'll die a good person.

16 Plus I made all humans equal.

17 Ninjas are inherently as good as pirates.

18 But they were deceived by Darwin and twisted by his Science.

19 That demon is the one you should be angry at."

20 "Fair enough."

21 "Sweet.

22 You shape up a little and I got your back.

23 But there's one more thing.

24 You must go forth and spread my word.

25 You must keep my faith alive.

26 For the Dark Lord Darwin will return and threaten mankind again.

27 His Science may destroy the world.

28 The Pastafarians must be prepared.

Please attend the Pastafarian Convention on August 9, 2024 at Best Western Plus Bradenton Gateway Hotel 2215 Cortez Road W, Bradenton, FL 34207

https://www.facebook.com/PastafarianLooseCanon/

The Book of Thinly-Veiled Modern Practice Agreements

1 One day, as the Flying Spaghetti Monster hovered in the clouds and looked down upon the modern world after the great
public revelation of Bobby Henderson (Pesto Be Upon Him), he noticed, yet again, the great lack of pirates.

2 This lack of pirates did make him quite peeved, and so he spoke unto the believers "What's up with the lack of pirates?

3 Did I not tell ye that the free-spirited pirates are the most beloved unto me, and instruct ye to pass on a very strong suggestion to the people that they dress in the blessed clothing?"

4 And the believers, many of whom were big whiners, did respond "But it's hard to dress up like a pirate in these modern times!

5 There are many unbelievers in the world, who do laugh and scorn our choice of clothing.

6 Their opinions would not matter but that their prejudices cause us great difficulty in keeping good work to put pasta on the table and not getting unnecessarily martyred."

7 "Hmm... I suppose a healthy diet of pasta is a pretty important observance in addition to the regalia, and that not getting killed is pretty important to you.

8 You must be able to work for the pasta you need, as I, like a forgetful fish owner, am not a terribly dependable provider of such things.

9 I understand that you must be respectful to societal norms in order to do that.

10 But there must be some way to recognize my followers, that I may bless them accordingly.

11 And how am I to know my followers if not by the omnipresence of flamboyant sea-faring style?"

12 The believers concurred with their delicious deity that the problem of how the deity may recognize the believer in hiding was very serious, and they promptly nominated members to a Divine Relations committee and accorded them task of solving it.

13 "We may have all true believers shave off their left eyebrows!" one committee member cried.

14 "Nay, such is crazy talk.

15 The believer may be recognized by a small calligraphic tattoo of another wench or pirate's name on their arse, as this clearly demonstrates he or she had achieved a drunken state of universal acceptance." said another.

16 And the third member spoke, "Well, that's awfully convenient for ye, isn't it Chuck?

17 Nay, the true Pastafarian in hiding shall don small symbols of their faith

under mildly pirate-inspired clothing such that
they may show the signs and share the style whilst not betraying mainstream society's tentative and volatile acceptance.

18 But let us also designate a day in each season specifically for the observance of that which is holy and wholesome as pasta
and piratedom, since we are so hidden at other times.

19 Let us stew the sauce for days on end, and give a portion to mark the entrances of sacred halls in which we gather as a place of free, open-hearted love and acceptance, as well as the possible location of a really awesome party.

20 Likewise, whenever and wherever we congregate, the doors shall be with marked with a banner of sauce color as a declaration of intent to our lord and invitation for all others to join in our revelry.

21 What are all your thoughts on such an arrangement?"

22 This seemed like a suitable suggestion to the members of the committee, and many nodded approvingly.

23 The FSM suddenly then spoke, giving the committee quite a scare as they had forgotten that he was watching the debate.

24 "Okay, that sounds like a good plan.

25 Let it be so.

26 But before I go, I would have ye remember: Thou must be respectable in public, but amongst yourselves and I there shall be no shame nor deceit, nor scandal nor scorn.

27 When the time comes that every man is free, all shall party and revel with their full, unconcealed piratitude."

28 And as it is written, so did all this come to pass.

29 Give or take a few minor details.

Please attend the Pastafarian Convention on August 9, 2024 at Best Western Plus Bradenton Gateway Hotel 2215 Cortez Road W, Bradenton, FL 34207

https://www.facebook.com/PastafarianLooseCanon/

A Pasta's Creed as passed to Solipsy

1 The True Believers did grow in number and in rank, and there was word spread that a great accounting should take place; a census should be taken and in that census should be counted all the men and the males among them, and all the women, and the females among them, and the children and the girls and the boys, and the infants.

2 And the leaders spoke up among the True Believers and declared that the numbers of the accounting of the census seemed to make sense not, for there was no accounting of the persons with indeterminate gender, and also of the persons who felt themselves to be gender mis-identified, and also, to count the children, then re-count the boy children and the girl children separately seemed to nearly double the numbers, not accounting for the gender non-specific.

3 And thus the Great Accounting of the True Believers did begin again, and this

time was it done by sorting the males and the females and the children and the gender non-specific, and the numbers were tallied and the numbers and ranks of the True Believers seemed to be relatively accurate and the land did feast upon the Holy Meal of the Pasta and Sauce and Orbs made of whatever Protein was the True Believers' Choice, and the Green Salad was dressed and served and The Tasty Garlic Bread passed.

4 The desired beverages were quaffed and there was great fellowship among the counted of the number and the rank of the True Believers.

5 Afterward, when the plates of the cleaned were gathered, the sweetened desserts of chocolate, dark or milk or white, or not of chocolate at all, but rather simply desserts as the True Believers did prefer, were passed.

6 And the True Believers gave great thanks and worship unto the Wise and Holy Flying Spaghetti Monster; the men and the women among them did rejoice,

and the children, both the male children and the female, and the infants did rejoice, and the gender non-specific.

7 All rejoiced and gloried in the Wisdom and Greatness of the One True Creator who made All That Is and Should Be Taught as Science.

8 Each and all among the number and the rank were sated; their hunger was sated and their thirst was quenched, and they were glad and tired.

9 For their numbers had been counted with relative accuracy and among them were many; 6354 were the men and 7364 were the women and 25366 were the children and 3907 were the gender non-specific regardless of age.

10 And they did look upon one another, and finally it was asked: What was the point of all that, then?

11 And came the answer from On High: "I'm not quite sure, but it was one heck of a party!"

12 At the rising of the sun the next morning, as the True Believers did

awaken, the men among them did arise, and the women and the children and the gender non-specific did arise, a great non-threatening yet thundering voice did call down from On High: "My Children Whom I Have Touched, Who Are Caressed By My Noodly Appendage, it is My wish for you that you live long and happily, and should have great good fun and gain much knowledge and use the brain I have given you and the free will I have given you and the discount shopping coupons and library cards I have given you."

13 And then a great sigh did rumble throughout the Earth and throughout the Sky and throughout all Creation.

14 "But," continued the Wiggly Lord, "I figure I ought to include for you a few specifics in case of emergency."

15 The holy scribes did run for their hammers and their chisels and their tablets of stone, and began to hammer furiously away in the ancient languages of the day.

16 They did endeavor to catch all the words of the Great Flying Spaghetti Monster as accurately as possible, and with few mistakes, for they wanted to please him, and make him happy.

17 They wanted not to incur His Wrath.

18 They did hammer and did pound and the chips of granite did collect at their feet and this transcribing they tried to do with much accuracy, for there was not, in those olden times of stone tablets, spell-check nor auto correct nor copy-paste.

19 They did live in dark times indeed, and hungered for the wisdom of the Holy Flying Pasta One.

20 Thusly they wrote, for this he spoke:

21 And it shall be that no eating of boogers shall occur in the market place, the classroom, the gas station, the fast-food restaurant, or the car while sitting at a red light, or in any other place.

22 This is His Noodly Word, and for to break it, the offender shall sacrifice three slices of mushroom pizza upside down

upon the altar of the offender's own coffee table.

23 There those slices shall remain until such time as do appear small gnats.

24 Then and only then is the offender considered cleansed of his booger-sin, and may dispose of the mushroomed slices, and shall sin no more.

25 His Holy Flying Spaghetti Monster shall not tolerate the owning of more than seven stuffed animals by a heterosexual man over the age of 25.

26 If such a man is found to be in possession of said offensive beasts, the beasts will be taken by the True Believers, and they shall be ritually sacrificed upon the garbage heap after much dismemberment.

27 The man shall then be taunted for a time not to exceed two minutes.

28 Then shall he hop on one foot for a full minute and be considered forgiven.

29 This sayeth our Lord and Noodle.

30 Should his girlfriend be the presenter of the beasts, she should be sternly told to

grow up, and instructed by the elder males among the True Believers about appropriate gifts for boyfriends, for yea and verily, she is freakin' clueless.

31 If the gifter be his Mother, it shall be explained to her that she is now the parent of a grown man, and ought consider gifts of cash instead.

32 Thus instructs The Wise and Meatbally.

33 The scratching of the most private parts or retrieval of the undergarments from the depths of the nether-regions shall be reserved for times when the True Believer has excused him/herself from the company of others, or such time as the True Believer wears the uniform of the team of a professional baseball player, and is on national television.

34 For the breaking of this sacred law, the penalty shall be that all those True Believers present and in observance shall loudly proclaim "Dude, quit scratching your (insert chosen offensive slang word

here)" while pointing at the unholy offender.

35 Equally shall this be done to all scratchers, disregarding genders.

36 In penance, the Disgraced True Believer must cover his face with both hands and excuse him/herself to the nearest restroom to wash up like a civilized person.

37 Then and only then shall the loving Noodles of the Holy One embrace him/her again.

38 The eating of pets, the True Believer shall not do, for verily and with most seriousness shall it be held an abomination.

39 Thou shall not eat of the hamster nor the gerbil, nor any other denizen of the Habitrail, neither of the cat nor its kittens, the dog nor its pups.

40 Neither shall thou partake of the flesh of the parakeet nor the iguana nor the goldfish nor any fish of the tank or decorative pond, for it is an abomination unto his Holy Jiggling Appendages.

41 Neither shall thee roast the flesh of pets from the store nor shelter, whether cuddly or annoying, for verily it is an abomination unto the Spaghetti Lord, and also of great repulsion to the sane.

42 Also it shall be held a deep abomination to partake of the flesh of the pets of thy neighbors, even if such pets do bark long and mightily throughout the night, disturbing the rest of the True Believer.

43 Even if the pets of thy neighbor's dig in thy yard and garden, or otherwise behave in ways which shall peeve thee, of them thou shall not eat.

44 Thou shall not grind them and mix their flesh with bread crumbs nor rice nor oats nor tasty seasonings of any kind, for it is an abomination.

45 Thou shall not bathe them in the sauces of any kind, nor shape them, thine own or thy neighbor's, into rounded form.

46 Thou shall not even consider them lowly unto the Atkins diet, for truly it is just plain sick.

47 For the breaking of this most high and holy law, the True Believer must submit to years of serious Psychiatric Counseling and agree to take such legal medications as are prescribed by a professional physician.

48 His Most Righteous Airborne Semolina Strands shall tolerate no petty traffic offenses from amongst the ranks of his True Believers.

49 Heed these words, O children of the Grain!

50 Verily, thou shall use thine turn indicators before such time as thou shall make a turn; before a left turn, and before a right turn, according to their kinds.

51 In both instances shall thee use them equally.

52 So too shall you, my True Believers, maintain assured clear distance from the drivers in front of thee, though they be morons who inhibit thine (only slightly over legally posted) speed.

53 For verily, thou art not the drivers of the cars in front of thee, nor can thou go

through them, as they are objects solid as granite, and should you hitteth them, the collision would be considered thine fault, and the payment of the deductible great.

54 Should you find yourself to be the victim of the heretic infidel, the tailer of the gate, thou are to make sure thou are doing the posted speed and maintain a temperament worthy of the True Believer of Your Extruded Nutritious Wheat-Based Lord.

55 You shall not mess with the idiot behind thee.

56 You shall not speed up for short distance only to slow down for short distance.

57 You shall not check to see if brakes work, neither the brakes of your car, nor the brakes of the jerkface behind thee.

58 Ye shall attempt to refrain from the stretching of the arm and the extension of the chosen finger, though it be mightily tempting, and The Lord Thy Glob doth quite understand, but still refrain if thee can, for it is better to pull over and keep

your life long, than to mess with a fool who may shorten it.

59 For the sake of thy Great Glob in Heaven, thou are not to be a fool who believes it to show great status among human kind to blast your chosen music throughout the streets for all to hear.

60 It is an abomination.

61 Not the choice of thine music is an abomination, mind you, but the deafening volume at which the idiot who blasts it doth blast it.

62 Blast not with the woofers nor the tweeters, nor anywhere throughout the midrange.

63 Blast not at the intersection, nor in the parking lot, nor through the neighborhood, nor in the presence of the person of one's chosen attraction, for yea and verily, please figure out that no one is impressed.

64 The Monster Who Has Rounded Orbs of Meat and Hovers in Heaven has blessed his Creation with music to make

his Creatures happy, music of all kinds that his Creatures may rejoice.

65 Be not an inconsiderate jackass who thinks everyone in the whole world is dying to hear the music of thine choice.

66 Trust the Big Monster on this one: they are not, and they do regard thee as most idiotic.

67 And another thing, and this doth peeve His Glorious Hovering Pasta no end: thou shall keep thy mind on thy driving and thine eyes on the road.

68 There shall be no long chatting on the phones of the cell, there shall no applying of the makeup to the face, no shaving of the beard, no reading of the map, the newspaper, the Romance novel, nor solving of the crossword puzzle.

69 There shall be no watching of the movie by thee as thou art driving.

70 There shall be no watching of the DVD, nor the VCR tape, nor the Television, neither VHF nor satellite.

71 Have thee lost thy freaking mind?

72 Verily should the sane among you, and the True Believers who wish to live long lives and see their children live long lives, seek to pass earthly laws against these abominations, and seek to have them duly enforced.

73 For those who escape Earthy justice, especially flat and bland beer doth await you in Heaven.

Penne and the Art of Pasta Making

Chapter 1

It was long ago that The Great Dark Age first began. The pasta had long left most kitchens, and the people fell into disrespect and pointlessness. Many things were lost to the age, and have yet to reappear, but with the light of the new pasta movement, they may yet do so. Here follows the account of its loss, and the account of its reacquisition.

Pasta had been long loved and respected in the world, especially within the countries of Italy and Japan, whose different styles of spaghetti were well-known to the enlightened, the pirates, and the midgets. People rejoiced in its simplicity and elegance; in its being a good source of starch for our diets. One such member of the enlightened, Elaine, both a pirate and a midget, revered the pasta above all others, and spent her time sailing the seven seas, spreading its tasty news far and wide, but whilst she was absent from her home port, trouble brewed there. It began with the invention of the first antipasto by a simple man. He thought that this was his greatest achievement, and expounded its virtues to his friends. They began making their own, and soon there was such a wide choice of antipasti, nobody knew what to do with it. The first pasta to disappear from menus due to the popularity of antipasti was fusilli, followed by tortellini, ravioli, and many others, until only linguini and spaghetti were left due to their relative simplicity. People began preferring the antipasti over all other meals, and before long, it was a rare occurrence to hear the ordering of pasta in any establishment, or see the kneading of flour and egg. In fact, so popular had it become, that its own adherents soon spread from Elaine's home port of Pastador, and travelled into the mainland of Italy. The scourge of antipasti spread like wild fire, and soon left the borders of Italy, spreading across Europe, and into the middle east, Asia, and Africa.

You see the major difference between pasta and antipasti were their methods of initial travel. Pasta, being holy, spread first by sea into the ports of the world, and by pirate ship at that. Antipasti, being unholy, spread first by land, and almost never touched any body of water if it could help it. The only way it reached the Americas was by people crossing the ice bridge between Siberia and Alaska, such was the hatred of water. If you were to look at a map, it would shockingly highlight this major difference quite plainly, and this is what made the antipasti travel with the speed it did. Whole communities that once revered pasta as Elaine did were now revering the antipasti and its deceptive simplicity. The knowledge of pasta soon was lost to many places, and in those places it survived, was only there as something different. Few were those who remembered its preparation.

Antipasti had not yet reached Japan due to its relative isolation by sea, but it was pressing at the borders of China and Korea, the pressure mounting until one day the dam broke, and the flood waters of antipasti poured forth across those lands, smothering all in the deluge of antipasti propaganda. The people had held onto the old and holy ways for as long as they could, but it was too much for them. The emperor of China had even built a large wall to keep out the antipasti proselytisers, but they managed to get around it with their perseverance. Eventually, it had taken over the world, with Japan being the only nation in which it was unheard of.

Chapter 2

Now at this time, Elaine was in Japan, the home of her mother (only her father was Italian), and was visiting family. It was a Friday, so she was dressed in pirate regalia as required, and enjoying the holy meal of noodles and fish balls with them, when the door suddenly burst open.

"Oh pirate Elaine, most revered prophet of the pasta incarnate, hear me, I beseech thee!" cried the man on his knees. Everyone was most shocked at this, as it was completely unexpected, but Elaine, being a kind and gentle woman, stood up and spoke to the man.

"Be not afraid of me, young man, for I will listen to thy words with humility and kindness," said Elaine, at which the man burst into forthright tears. Elaine dried them with her piratical sleeves and looked at him tenderly. "Tell me what ails thee, most faithful friend."

"I have just returned from a journey, and was refused entry into every Chinese port along the coast. When I asked them why, they said that it was because I had not accepted the antipasti as reverent, and not shunned the wickedness of pasta." At this a gasp of shock spread around the table as a sense of foreboding spread through all present.

Could this be what I had feared beyond all else? thought Elaine as she paced to and fro. Could this be the end of the world, as foretold by St. Pa Stasor my ancestor? This greatly troubled her, and caused wrinkles to form on her perfect brow. "I must meditate on this, and beseech the FSM for His most holy guidance," she said at last.

Making her apologies and leaving the house of her relatives, she went away to a quiet place she liked to use for contemplation, tears running down her smooth cheeks. As she sat thinking on the FSM, all she could see were images of a beer volcano and a stripper factory. Suddenly, the realisation came to her what the FSM was saying; that she needed to go where the grog and the strippers were! She sped to the port to speak to the pirates assembled in the bars, taverns and brothels there. She needed to confirm this before acting, but everywhere she went, the story was the same. There were even pirates from Spain there, who had encountered the same message of antipasti everywhere they went. This was not what she wanted to hear, but it was what she knew in her pre-frontal cortex was true.

The mood was dark in the docks, very dark, and the rising air of despair was beginning to get to her, so she decided to engage in decent piratical activities to clear her head, and allow her the time to think of her plan. After entering Kanagawa-san's Grog & Stripper Sanctum, Elaine took a booth seat, and ordered a jug of their strongest ale. At first she was sipping, but before long, Elaine was quaffing and feeling the effects, which aroused her in other ways. Signalling to Kanagawa-san that she wanted company, one of the male strippers approached and sat next to her. She wondered whether to apologize, send him away, and ask for one of the female strippers instead, but at that point she could not be bothered to do so. Needless to say, she made the best of what she had, and eventually left feeling satisfied in more ways than one.

Heading for her ship, she spied her crew ambling back from their night's pleasantries, all looking the worse for wear as usual, but with an undercurrent of fear. The news had begun to spread! It was then that a plan began formulating in her mind.

Chapter 3

The pirate Elaine knew that a dark age had befallen the world, and that Japan was its last best hope for enlightenment. Over the coming months, more and more pirates sailed to Japan with many refugees from the enlightened peoples of the world. With such a large number of people arriving, the taverns and hostelries were soon full, so a grand effort was made to accommodate them, with buildings of bamboo appearing wherever there was space. The pirates, for the first time in their lives, forsook their ships for land, and although this was difficult, it was a necessity for them. Gone were their traditional short swords in favour of the katana, the weapon of the Samurai. The pirates also took on some of the dress of the Samurai, modelling their hats and clothing, but being pirates, the old ways were never truly lost. Eventually, the pirates ended up with a dress that was partway between what they used to wear, and the dress of the Samurai. Even the katanas of many were put aside in places of honour, and replaced with a weapon that resembled it, but was also similar in design to the short sword. This was thenceforth known as the cutlass, which was like a curved short sword.

The pirates felt an affinity with the Samurai, as their codes of honour were quite similar, and before long the pirate code evolved into a new version of Bushido, their central tenets being:-

Rectitude (義) - Uphold the way of the Most Holy Pasta and Piracy.

Courage (勇) - Defend the Most Holy Pasta and Piracy in all situations.

Benevolence (仁) - Give freely of the Most Holy Pasta and Piratical advice and assistance.

Respect (礼) - Respect the diversity of pasta, and the code of the Pirate.

Honesty (誠) - Never lie about pasta, or about being a Pirate.
Honour (名誉) - Honour the code, and all that it stands for.

Loyalty (忠義) - Never leave a fellow Pirate in their hour of need.

In fact, so taken were many of the pirates with the Samurai, and vice versa, they took to spending time learning each others' arts, so that it got to the stage where you could tell neither one from the other if they were appropriately dressed. Japan was dramatically changed by this, as were its visitors, and Japan entered a new era of enlightenment, where peace reigned supreme, and co-operation drove the people forward.

The pirates, as they arrived, brought with them all the recipes for pasta that they could, and it was to Elaine that these were taken, for she had taken upon herself to write them all down in a great book to rival that of Pastucius himself. Many pirates set sail again to explicitly collect any recipes that could be found, along with any of the enlightened that had survived the scourge of the antipasti, which became known as The Great Search. More was saved than Elaine would have thought possible, amongst which were some of the greatest thinkers of her day. Most were from the East, as it was easier for them to get to Japan than it was for those from Africa or Europe, but there was still hope, as little enclaves of freethought and pasta still survived throughout the world, although their number was few.

Chapter 4

Reports began to file in about the state of
health of the adherents of the antipasti, as
a plague began to sweep the lands. The
greatly decreased amount of starch, and
therefore carbohydrates, in the diets of the
world had devastating effects. People
began lacking glucose and other sugars,
byproducts of eating pasta, which led to a
slowing of the brain's functions,
irritability, and exhaustion. The people
couldn't think as quickly as before, which
combined with the irritability, led to wars,
but these wars were short-lived due to the
lethargy. This caused more local
outbreaks of lethargic violence, with most
not bothering, but what damage was
caused was almost the cause of the end of
civilisation. The long-term effect of
lethargy meant that not enough food was
being grown, repairs were not made to
infrastructure or housing, and the people
became emaciated. Birth rates also
dropped dramatically, and what used to

be once thriving cities, full of the hustle and bustle of life, became virtual ghost towns, a few poor souls wandering slowly along the streets.

Elaine knew that her efforts must be redoubled, and that something had to be done soon, but the forces of the antipasti were strong; maybe even too strong for her. A great meeting was called, gathering together all the pirate ship captains, the Samurai clan leaders, the greatest thinkers of Japan, and all the enlightened amongst the Japanese and the refugees from the rest of the world. The meeting began with all who had news of the outside world telling the assembly what was going on. Many there did not truly understand the scale of the issue until then, and many a gasp was heard. Once the news had began recounted to all, a great silence fell upon the assembly, as if something profound was about to happen, but it wasn't long before one captain voiced his own solution.

"We need to look at the teachings of Pastucius to find our way out of this mess," he said, looking around him. "When affairs cannot be carried on to success, piracy and pasta do not flourish," he began, "to govern by virtue, let us compare it to the North Star: it stays in its place, while the myriad stars wait upon it. The expectations of the pirate depend upon diligence; the pirate that would perfect his work must first sharpen his cutlass. We must await the outcome of this, then attend to the solution!"

This caused a great stir among the people, as many murmured partial agreement with him. At this, a Samurai clan leader stepped forward, saying, "But this is to do nothing in the face of adversity. Wise are your words, fellow enlightened one, as you advise caution and patience, two great virtues in anyone, yet you advocate inaction. We need to follow Pas Tza and be extremely subtle, even to the point of formlessness. Be extremely mysterious, even to the point of soundlessness. Thereby we can be the director of our opponent's fate. If we confront them with annihilation, they will then survive; plunge them into a deadly situation, they will then live. When people fall into danger, they are then able to strive for victory. Only this can lead us to victory, and bring enlightenment back to our world!"

Once again, there was a murmur, greater this time due to the rousing words of the Samurai, an advocate of all-out warfare on the antipasti scourge. The assembly fell silent once again, contemplating the wise words just heard, when Elaine walked
into the silent throng. All eyes fell upon her, as she stood there, head bowed and eyes closed. It appeared as if she was meditating whilst standing up, one of the skills of an experienced pirate captain, until her eyes suddenly fluttered open.

"Sistren and brethren. Pirate and Midget. Samurai and philosopher. We are enlightened, one and all. We hear the words of wisdom from our fellows, and agree with both, yet we are torn between one and the other. Did Pas Tza not say "It is only the enlightened ruler and the wise general who will use the highest intelligence of the army for the purposes of spying, and thereby they achieve great results"? This we have done in our endeavours. Did not Pastucius say "A superior pirate is modest in their speech, but exceeds in their actions"? This we have yet to do. But there is another way. A path to true enlightenment that each of us knows, yet has somehow forgotten. I speak of The Way of Penne." Elaine stood there, looking at the open mouths of astonishment from many of those assembled, and smiled inwardly. She had brought them all to where she needed them. Many days and weeks she had spent meditating on this issue, seeing elusive images from the FSM, and maybe many that were not, but it was the act itself that finally made her realise what was needed.

"The journey of a thousand leagues must begin with a single sail. The ocean is like a mirror, you see? Smile and your crew smile back. Give a pirate pasta and you feed them for a day. Teach a pirate to make pasta, and you feed them for a lifetime!" she told them. A murmur began once again, which rose to a tumult of applause and agreement. Calling for silence once again, Elaine explained to them all, "I have finished the finest book ever written. Within its sacred cover is every known recipe for pasta. This must be copied and spread. We have the pirates, we have the ships, but this is not going to be an easy undertaking. It must spread from port to port, from country to country, until the whole world is in a new age of enlightenment. We must not stop. We must not falter. Step by step we will take back this world, and reclaim it for Him!"

The audience erupted once again, but louder than before. Elaine's empassioned speech had aroused them all, and together they were going to take back what was lost.

Chapter 5

It was The Time of Copy Pasta in which the sacred Book of Pasta, as it had come to be known, was transcribed by many into the tongues of the world. This was such an undertaking, that almost everyone not involved in preparing the fleet was used, from the making of the pages from rice and olive tree wood, the making of the ink by the milking of squid, to the transcribing itself. Millions of books were eventually produced for the effort, and were loaded onto the ships, now repaired, scrubbed clean (even the bilges), and ready to sail out into the world. A new breed of pirate had evolved in this time, more spiritual, more forthright, and far deadlier than before, regaled as they were in their new finery, replete with cutlass and pointy hat.

Elaine had worked tirelessly for the 10 years it took to prepare everything, co-ordinating the transcription in The Time of Copy Pasta, organising the refit of the pirate fleet, and formulating the plans for the second coming of pasta to the world. Many were the sacrifices made by Elaine, and big was the hardship, but by meditation, not to mention the consumption of every type of pasta in the book, she made it through, looking and feeling healthier than she had ever done. The same was true of most of the enlightened folk, as they endeavoured to make right what was wrong.

Thus The Time of Kneading drew near, when the preparation was finished and the spreading of pasta was to begin. A great assembly was called for all who could attend, and they did gather in the greatest meeting hall ever built. Millions attended to see pirate Elaine speak in what was to be the seminal speech of the year.

"Sistren and Brethren. Pirates and Midgets. Samurai. We, the enlightened ones, have worked hard these past years in preparation for this day. No longer shall we see the world suffer through the tyrannies and inequities of the antipasti. Long have we laboured by night and by day. Much is the pasta we have eaten, and many are the Holy Meals we have shared. Today is a new beginning. Today we start anew. Today we embrace The Art of Penne. Do not think of what you do, just react, for reaction without thinking is what is needed for Him to take us over and touch us. There are many here who agree that we must act, but do not fully agree with the methods, and for listening to me I say thank you, but I shall now show you all that we are both blessed and touched by Him," Elaine told the assembly.

Looking around from the very centre of the people, she asked everyone to close their eyes and empty their minds. Slowly, circle by circle, the people did so, and they were instantly filled with a peace so calm as to make them think they were flying. "Merge your mind with cosmic space, integrate your actions with myriad forms," suggested Elaine, as the assembled people began swaying slightly, when suddenly everyone heard a kind yet booming voice in their heads.

"HEAVEN AND EARTH COME FROM THE SAME NOODLE AS MYSELF. ALL APPENDAGES AND I BELONG TO ONE WHOLE." The room shook suddenly, as everyone felt a pressure against their person, and the entire assemblage shrunk by exactly 2.54 centimetres. He had not only touched them with His Noodly Appendages, but had showed them favour by pushing them towards midgethood. A cry of joy went up as the assembled people rejoiced that He had chosen to show Himself to them.

As the meeting came to a close, Elaine assigned ports for the enlightened to travel to, the details of which were already written and placed close to the pirate captains. When asked where she would be travelling to, Elaine replied, "If you want to climb a mountain, begin at the top. I shall be going to Pastador, the heart of the antipasti menace!" A hush followed as many realised how dangerous a part of the mission she had chosen for herself, and many offered to take her place, beseeching her not to risk her life so. "I would rather sink to the bottom of the sea for endless aeons than seek liberation through all the antipasti of the universe," replied Elaine, "I shall go with my fearless crew and spread word there myself, for to no other would I assign this most risky of missions. Go in peace, oh enlightened ones. RAmen!"

"RAmen," echoed the people. The meeting was now over, and the real work was about to begin.

Chapter 6

The journey was long and arduous as the crew did all they could to keep their spirits up. Much dried pasta and noodles had been packed, along with meatballs and fish balls, not to mention the large amount of grog. Many months it took to get to even the Cape of Good Hope, with many more to travel up Africa to the Gibraltar straits, and into the Mediterranean sea. Elaine did her best to maintain high spirits in her crew, but the more they saw of that state of the people whenever they were forced to anchor the ship off the coast and row ashore, the more depressed they became. Pirate Elaine ended up steering a course well clear of the coast, as she knew the effect it was having. She also knew that there were many other ships sailing for the places they anchored near, so was content in the fact that soon the mission would begin in earnest.

There were ships sent to every major and minor port on the coasts of Africa, the Americas, Europe, Asia, and Australasia, with specialist missions to find every enclave of enlightenment, few that they were. The work would be difficult, but using The Art of Penne should make it instinctual, not to mention allowing the enlightened to get closer to Him and His Divine Pastenance. The closer they were to their goal, the more they meditated, until they were able to be once again at peace with themselves and the sea.

The day came when the port of Pastador was spied from the crow's nest, and a hush took itself upon the crew. Captain Elaine was on deck with her spyglass, looking out towards the land, spying for a place to anchor that would be hidden from view. Suddenly she spotted it, and yelled, "Make for St. Pa Stasor's Point, and enter Linguini Cove, first mate Royston." This was obeyed, and the ship was steered towards the relative safety of the harbour. The currents were good, as if moved by an invisible force, and they were soon hidden from view of the mainland. Dropping anchor, they started unloading the crates and rowing them ashore. It took them a while, but that was finally done, and they made their plans to steal into the town at night.

As the moon rose, a procession of pirates lugging crates left the vicinity of the cove, with the captain and first mate heading towards the heart of the town, and hence the heart of antipastidom, and the crew heading to the eating and drinking establishments, not to mention the brothels and strip joints, those hallowed halls of learning. Each carried their fair share of copies of The Book of Pasta, distributing them in secret to the needy and the lost until they needed to come back to the cove for more. Many were not distributed, though, as they were being saved for those further inland.

As Elaine and Royston reached the heart of town, they were stopped dead in their tracks by the sight of a temple to Antipasti. Never before had anyone built a temple to pasta or the power of the FSM, yet here was this monstrosity in the heart of her beloved home! Before leaving the shadows, Elaine made sure that her robe hid her raiment properly, advising Royston to do the same. Across the town square did pirate Elaine walk, although her movements belied her purpose that night, for she stooped a little, and shuffled as she walked, appearing as if one of the antipasti faithful. This way did she gain entry past the lethargic guards of the temple, and passage to the inner sanctum. There the strongest adherents to the antipasti lay. This was the battle Elaine had prepared herself for all those years, as foretold to her by the

FSM in a vision of her dressed in drab garb, as she was now, standing in a temple devoted to wasting away.

Standing there as she was, she attracted the attention of one of the priests who approached her, making the sign of the antipasti at her as if in welcome. "I come to seek your wisdom, sirs," said Elaine in as tired a voice as she could manage, "I have travelled many leagues to be here, and seek that which you can tell me."

The priest seemed puzzled by her language and intonation. "Have you, my dear?" he replied. "Tell me that which you seek, and I shall provide it for you." Clapping his hands lazily, he summoned a servant with a tray of antipasti, proffering it to Elaine.

"No," she said, refusing the proffered dish, "I do not partake of this filth." The priest stood back, aghast. Never before had he been spoken to this way. "I come preaching health and forgiveness from Him on high. I come with a gift," she said to him, reaching inside her robe and brandishing The Book of Pasta as if some form of talisman. Taking one quick look at the title of the book, realisation dawned upon him that this was not some joke, or indeed a cruel one. This was what their order had worked so hard to destroy all those years ago. By this stage, all the inhabitants of the room began to realise what was going on between their leader and the strange, drably-dressed woman. To see a woman in here was rare for them, as theirs was strictly a patriarchal society, the ways of the woman having been reduced to childrearing and housekeeping long ago.

Whispers were made, and word went out of what was happening inside the temple, and they had soon attracted quite an audience of lethargic onlookers, eager to see something different. The tension was palpable. "Let us take this outside," suggested Elaine, "I want more people to witness your downfall." Eagerly agreeing to this through his overconfidence, the high priest and all assembled moved from the inner sanctum towards the front doors to the temple, spilling out into the moonlit night. Many had gathered here as well; such a sight that had not been seen since the old days before the downfall and the dark times.

Elaine and the high priest made their way to the middle of the square, the crowd parting for them slowly. Looking round, Elaine saw that most of the faces were relatively young, the old being too weak to move much at all. A circle had opened in the middle of the square, allowing the two of them in as a hush fell upon the crowd. When the two were face to face in the stillness of the night, the Patriarch of antipasti expounded so-called virtues of antipasti to Elaine and the people, weaving his lies so very well. He mentioned the healing properties of the water used in cooking antipasti, stating that when watered down it became far more potent. The people ate these lies like so much antipasti, yet Elaine remained calm and passive throughout the tirade.

Elaine started clapping slowly, emphasising her disdain at his words, slowly building up to a speed unseen and unheard in these lands for many a year. A quiet and not-so-lethargic murmur ran through the crowd. Is this it? Is this the beginning of the end for the antipasti? she thought, moving her hands slowly but surely to the clasp on her cloak. Suddenly Elaine whipped her cloak from her body, revealing her regalia in its full splendour. The priests cowed on the ground at the sight of her magnificence and beauty, at last removed from its cover. "Hear me, you people of Pastador. Once I lived among you as one of you, and I was accepted. My father's family once lived here, but although my mother came from a different land many leagues away, and you were kind to her as any adherent of the One True Pastenance should be. Do you not recognise one of your own? A few gasps were heard from those brave enough to gaze upon her. Elaine removed her cutlass and a copy of The Book of Pasta from their places on her person, raising them towards Him in supplication.

"So I tell you, sistren and brethren, listen unto His teachings, for only through them does real wisdom flow. These are the words of Him to His people." The people began watching ever more closely. "Do you not remember Him saying to us, "I'd really rather you didn't build multimillion-dollar temples...when the money could be better spent ending poverty, curing diseases, living in peace, loving with passion and lowering the cost of cable"? Do you not remember the other commandments passed down to Captain Mosey on Mount Salsa? Remember to keep your mind alive and free without abiding in anything or anywhere." The throng was suddenly and thoroughly enlightened as to the meaning of those words, even the priests were in tears at the realisation of what they had done.

That night, in the square, a feast was made of the Most Holy Meal of spaghetti and meatballs. A sudden transformation occurred, as everyone suddenly felt their energy coming back after so long without any. The Holy Meal had cured them of their ills. A great pressure was felt my all present, too, as if they were being touched heavily, although i'm sure that you'll be unsurprised to hear that all present shrunk by exactly 2.54 centimetres that night. Many books were distributed by Elaine and her crew, and some began copying them straight away, ensuring that they would spread far and wide once again. All who looked upon Elaine that night fell in love with her totally. Such was the feeling spreading throughout everyone, that Elaine allowed a tear to roll down her perfect cheek before its glistening beauty fell from her chin to the floor below. It was at that very spot that an olive tree was planted in memory of that night, which continues to flourish and grow to this day.

Chapter 7

The coming years were long and arduous. After setting straight the people of Pastador that night, a wave of love and pasta spread through the port and surrounding town. Soon, The Book of Pasta started to spread far and wide into the land, taken by the landlubbers to their neighbours and beyond. Elaine and her crew eventually set sail once the foundation of the new age was set, and moved along the coast, spreading the love of the FSM to all they met. They found that many were crying out for help in this time of great need, and were only too grateful to accept what was given to them. It was also the time of great shortening, as each and every one of them shrunk by exactly 2.54 centimetres as they were touched by His Noodly Appendages. Rains of pasta sauce were seen all over the land, as these were the tears of the FSM, so touched was He by the people coming back.

The story was the same the world over, although others had tougher times with their enlightenment mission. In these places a more subtle approach was needed, as the book was subtly introduced to those with a more open mind, who then spread it onwards. It took many years for the book to gain a foothold along most of the coast, and many years for it to penetrate into the heat of the lands, even with the speed it moved at. People first had to cook and eat of the pasta recipes in the book to be healed, and for many the healing was a very long process, but once done, the pastaful made copies of the book and gave them to others.

We still see the scars of this dark age now, as there are those who refuse to eat of the Holy Meal, but the work goes on and the book circulates. Elaine is a hero of the pirate world, and the dark age altered her beyond reckoning, but she was not all that was altered. The pirate we know today would not exist without the ways of the Samurai and their Bushido code, nor would they look like they do without this influence. The great wall built in China to stop the advance of antipasti is still there as a stark reminder of what once was and what could once happen again. The secret pirates watch tirelessly for this menace to arise again, safeguarding both the original book and the bones of their most revered Elaine.

Please attend the Pastafarian Convention on August 9, 2024 at Best Western Plus Bradenton Gateway Hotel 2215 Cortez Road W, Bradenton, FL 34207

https://www.facebook.com/PastafarianLooseCanon/

The Pastalamentations of Father Jerome

Book One

1 O Lord of Starchy Tentacles, hear thy repentant servant in exile:

2 I sit on the bank of this dry river; yea, I cry out to thee in heart-rending pastalamentations; but lo, my tears shall surely cause the river to flow afore they may soften Thine heart and make Thee relent.

3 Woe is me! Thou hast exiled me into this land of heathenistic Tacobeanias; and woe unto them, for they worship untasty gods. But let their beans be upon their own heads.

4 Thou sayest, O Lord FSM, that I shall go forth and mingle with the heathens and break Spaghetti with them in atonement for my sins?

5 Yea, therefore I shall go forth and eat Thy Noodly Meals in public places, and in the company of loose women,

fornicators and others who reject Thine Hallowed Substance; yea, I shall go among the sinners of Phoenix so that they may observe my ways and thereby learn to consume Thine Hallowed Delicious Meal. Yea!

6 Behold, in my search for Thine Holy Pasta I had entered "Antonio's Fine Food ala Italiano." At least so proclaimed the unevenly flashing neon sign above the entrance door.

7 And in the poorly-lit room I saw tables which were gaudily covered with red-white checkered cloth. My heart rejoiced. Pasta be praised, for is not Our Lord Spaghetti with Meatballs of Italian-Pastafarian persuasion? Surely, I shall find my Lord Pasta in this house.

8 And, lo, I rested my ass upon a vinyl-covered chair and waited for the high priest to come and arrange for Thee to appear in Thine Holy Form of Spaghetti and Sauce and Meatballs.

9 Someone emerged from the darkness of the eatery and accosteth me. "Stranger,

what wishest thou of me? Mayhap taco salad; bean tacos; sour cream chicken enchiladas" Thus spoke the high priest of that heathen eatery.

10 "None of these–nor none of those," I answered in indignation. "Only Spaghetti and Meatballs, and all smothered in His Sauce; for I am an orthodox Pastafarian. And make it pronto!"

11 So I instructed this false priest of my wishes, albeit in the awful dialect of Tacobeania, a lingo that resembles Español.

12 And thus spoke he: "O stranger, thou must know this: Antonio's joint hath changed ownership more than twice; I strive to serve foods which are clean in the eyes of our own regional gods 'Taco and Enchilada.' But I wish your God 'Pasta' (sneer, snicker) a very happy landing."

13 "But, stranger unto our land and customs," he then added, "my heart is not made of river rock. Mayhap the harlot–uh, cook, Juanita, can find a handful of

forgotten spaghetti in some nook or cranny; behold, I may yet persuade her to cook a sauce for thee…say, doest thou like beans?" So spoke the heathen who served unto the false gods 'Taco' and 'Enchilada.' Woe unto them.

14 And behold! The parquet floor shifted and all chairs and tables trembled. Oh, fearful sight! A mountain of flesh came unto my table; and–behold–it was the part-time cook: Juanita.

15 And such were the consequences which had resulted from the ingestion of unholy foods: she was as broad as she was tall, and thus her form appeared to be spherical.

16 The words of an English bard came to mind: "Marry, sir, she is the kitchen-wench, and all grease; and I know not what use to put her to, but to make a lamp of her, and run from her by her own light."

17And behold, her protruding belly supported two bowls, and those bowls she topped off with the lower pair of her four enormous breasts. In her entirety she fully resembled the legendary four-breasted harlot of Phoenix. And woe! that she was.

18 And lo, from her first bowl she served me a dish of ersatz-pasta and hamburger helper and salsa. Behold, the second bowl was empty.

19 And she stood near my right side and waited. And I ate while she stood there with the second bowl, the one that contained nada.

20 And it came to pass that I had finished the heathens' blasphemous substitute for Holy Pasta and Sauce and Meatballs.

21 Lo, the mountain of flesh held her empty bowl beneath my chin; and I understood this to be her subtle hint that I should place a substantial offering into that vessel; therefore I searched my purse for some loose shekels, whereupon she frowned; and then she spoke:

22 "Fie, stranger, it is not thy monetary reward that I wouldst cherish; but pray,

why pukest and fartest thou not? Hath my food not been to thy liking?"

23 I refused to oblige her, and thus she retreated with nothing more than one clean bowl in her hand. (Lord, who can understand these heathens' ways?)

24 Lord Pasta! I cry out to Thee for deliverance from exile; for I crave Thy Pasta; Thy Sauce and Thy Meatballs. I have been good; am I not Thine obedient Pastafarian? Exile me, O Pasta, if Thou wilt, to Chicago; or to Cleveland; even to Milwaukee; anywhere; for there, Thy Pastafarians shall serve Thee well.

Book Two

1 Woe unto me, for I still live in the land of heathenish Tacobeanians. Verily, the displeasure of Our Lord FSM is still upon me.

2 Behold, I consort with one of their most-vile denizens: the aforementioned four breasted harlot of Phoenix; yea.

3 And lo, it came to pass that she entered into my kitchen (for she desired to learn about my Lord Pasta and His Condiments and His Meatballs).

4 And, Lord Pasta forgive me, I ogled her four stupendous breasts in amazement, for never before had my eyes beheld more than three breasts on any female body. Lord, for viewing that abomination, yea, I rightly deserve fifty lashes with Thy Noodle.

5 And it came to pass that she desired to learn how to make Thy Blessed Meatball, and so I shewed her how to prepare Thy Balls of Protein.

6 "Much-esteemed four-breasted harlot of Phoenix," I said unto this heathen, "first thou takest of the following:

7 One pound of hallowed ground beef; 1/2 cup of bread crumbs; one egg that thou first beatest lightly; ½ cup of sacred Spaghetti Sauce; 1 tsp of salt and 1 tsp of onion flakes. Then thou mixest the entire Holy Shebang and shapest It into 1 inch Holy Balls. Thou bakest His Sacred Balls

in a pan, in a preheated oven at 400 degrees, but for no more and no less than 20 minutes shalt thou bake Them. "

8 "O Master of thine own oven," spoke the four-breasted harlot of Phoenix. "Woe is me, for I have kneaded one of my contact lenses into the Holy Mix. See? it lieth here upon the surface of His Meatball."

9 "Behold," I replied, "do not distress thyself, gracious harlot. Cook this, thine Holy Ball and consume It along with the lens; for then Our Vision-enhanced Holy Meatball shall fully see thine innermost self as He passeth through thee. Yea, He will see everything, including the taco."

Book Three

1 Woe unto the four-breasted harlot of Phoenix! Her filthiness is in her skirts; alas, clean laundry hath not yet been delivered to my abode; for here she now resideth. But who am I to look for flaws in her? Behold; I am not the cleanest

myself.

2 Yea, even she is an abomination in the eyes of her people, and she existeth at a pariah level equal to mine; but she pitieth me, for I am a foreign lowlife here in Tacobeania.

3 Behold, she inquired: "Wouldst thou not show me, O master of thine electric oven, how even I, a common harlot, might make fine spaghetti from plain dough?"

4 "Hush, gentle harlot," thus spoke I. "Spaghetti derives from Holy Dough; therefore thou must, when thou speakest of Lord Pasta, capitalize the first letter in His Name, yea, and even those which are found in all adjectives and all such which stand afore It; for they greatly serve to glorify His Holy Doughy Entity; verily, such reverence pleases Him mightily."

5 "But let us not dally, for we must make Spaghetti from Holy Dough, but no more and no less than is required to sate the hunger of one Pastafarian and his heathen consort."

6 Behold! Thou takest two cups of flour and two eggs, no more, no less; for so it is written. Thou addest one T. of salt; next thou takest ½ cup of water at room temperature and addest it to the previous. Thou mixest it well until it is on the firm side; it shall be neither soft nor hard. And, behold; there is The Holy dough.

7 Then thou kneadest His Holy Dough on a well-floured board, and then thou shalt cover It for some time.

8 Take thy knife, oh, harlot, and cut His Starchy Dough into manageable sections. Well done!

9 Next thou rollest each of These Doughy Portions into a Holy Ball.

10 Behold, now thou rollest each Ball into a Sacred Circle of no more than 1/2 cubit in diameter; and His Thickness shall be between ¼ inch to ½ inch.

11 Next thou takest thine Holy Disks and rollest Them through the rollers of thy Spaghetti machine for the desired final thickness.

12 Yea, now thou runnest His Holy Circles through thy purified Spaghetti cutters and hangest His Strands up to dry"

13 Great Pasta! Behold, that heathen woman hath placed Thine Holy Spaghetti into a seething pot of water and cooked it for two hours.

14 And woe, she said unto me: "Ees theees whadda cooked spaghettees shou'd look like, huh?"

15 Woe, all Thy Strands have jelled into a pasty two-inch layer. Woe, and woe! she then proceeded to slice a pocket into this glutinous lump and defiled it with pinto beans and such.

16 And the four-breasted harlot of Phoenix found Thy desecrated representation to be exquisite in flavor; and woe, she renameth the 'The Mighty Gordita.'

17 Lord Pasta, my heart is heavy; my body no longer lusteth for the harlot; it desireth only Thee. Besides, she is toooooo mucha grande for me. Yea

Book Four

1 Oh Lord Pasta, here is a word for the wise: "Hell hath no fury like a woman scorned."

2 Woe is me, for the harlot of Phoenix hath broken my teeth with gravel stones and creased my pate, for I had shewn her the door.

3 And I said unto her: "Harlot, thou breakest my teeth, thou cuttest off my hair; now my strength and my hope is perished."

4 And it came to pass that she mumbled: "Whatever! thou foreign ninny…" And behold, then she rearranged her breasts and, with that out of the way, she gracefully rolled down the porch steps and right out of my life. (Keep on rolling, rolling)

5 Lord Pasta is merciful in His mysterious ways; hath He not released me from bondage to that heathen behemoth?

6 Yea, and now I shall go forth and purchase a can of His Preserved

Representational Body, for I need to regain my strength; if such is His will. RAmen.

Book Five

1 Lo and woe! Above all, how much longer, Lord Pasta, must I remain in the land of the Tacobeanians?
 2 My tears have filled the previously dry river bed, the one which our heathens now call 'The River of Tears.' For a river of tears it becomes each time thy servant crieth out to Thee for deliverance from exile. Yea! Yea, for such is my great sorrow.
 3 Behold, I have rent into pieces my finest Gucci shirt and strewn ashes upon my pate. I have given my Lucchese alligator boots to a hobo. What else wouldst Thou that I should offer unto Thee and the local trash heap? My Calphalon Anodized 8-pc. Cookware set?

Book Six

Written after his deliverance from exile and ensuing gluttony.

1 Behold, Lord Pasta, I still cry out to Thee. Mine eyes are once more filled with tears. Woe is me, for I am in gastrointestinal distress: My bowels are troubled; I am bloated; my pyloric valve hath closed up well-nigh permanently; woe, my acid reflux condition hath reached hitherto unknown discomfort levels; I cry out in pain: O FSM, make it feel all better! Woe! woe! even my cats think that I am so full of S* (Spaghetti, that is)!

2 Thy smell of garlic and green pepper is still upon me. Woe, woe unto me! The acidity of Thy Plum Tomatoes eats away the protective lining of my stomach; yea, and Thy Meatballs smote me mightily last night; for they contained a pinch of finely grated onions and pepper and salt and Italian seasonings; woe is me! Alas, only

the makers of Chico's Italian Hot Sausages would know for certain what all had been stuffed into their casings; for such mighty meaty links I had (probably blasphemously) added into Thy Simmering Holy Mix and allowed them to fornicate with Thy Meatballs. Woe is me, for even Thy Sauce hath contained too many of Thy Thrice-blest Spices.

3 And woe, through my fault, through my fault, through my most-grievous fault, I overindulged in Thy Simmered Condiment which I had so generously poured over Thy Noodly Strands. Mayhap I should have partaken only in the consumption of Thy Farinaceous Appendages? Woe unto me for my reckless self-abandonment to culinary pleasure. Cursed be my palate; yea, I curse Thee and Thy host of taste buds.

4 And woe, woe, woe; although Thy Scrumptiousness hath only been a brief foretaste of Thy Pasta Heaven, alas, I fear that I shall enter into Thy Kingdom with all mine earthly afflictions and therewith

be doomed to eternally toggle between immeasurable delights and hellish torments. Woe is me ad nauseam.

The Book of Jeff

Chapter 1

1 Once upon a time in the holy land of New Jersey, a worried, young Pastafarian named Steve went to seek reassurance and solace from the leader of his congregation.

2 "Captain Jeff, Captain Jeff!" he cried.

3 "Every day I see more news that the scientists are finding more evidence for their theories.

4 Theories that contradict our beliefs!

5 I fear the Dark Lord Darwin is trying to tempt me with his reason.

6 I fear his power in this world is growing and the Pastafarians are doomed.

7 You must do something to stop him and his science!"

8 "Uh...

9 Dude, you give me way too much credit," said Captain Jeff. "I may be a leader of a congregation, but I'm actually pretty incompetent.

10 I'm not nearly powerful enough to smite Darwin, but don't worry, our savior is coming.

11 Soon the Pastafarian messiah will be sent by the Flying Spaghetti Monster to vanq
uish Darwin."

12 "Seriously?" asked Steve.

13 "You bet your ass, dude," replied Captain Jeff.

14 "Will he be the son of the FSM?"

15 "Maybe," answered Captain Jeff, "He does get around.

16 But he doesn't really have to be the son of the FSM or even the FSM Himself in human form for him to be a good guy."

17 "I see," said Steve, "Can you tell me more?"

18 "Sure," said Captain Jeff, "Just sit back and I'll do some prophesizing."

Chapter 2

1 "The messiah will come soon, probably sometime in the next few years. He will go by many names:

2 Juicetaker, Juicegiver, Vasudera Torrent, Peacefulsongs, Nancy Delia, Buttlicking22 and Eric Whitfield.

3 He won't look like what we'd expect.

4 He will not be a midget, but he will be quite short.

5 He will not have peg leg or a hook for a hand, and there will be no parrot on his shoulder.

6 Oh, and he won't be a fictional character, he'll be very real.

7 His teachings might be a little unexpected too, at least for some Pastafarians.

8 He will promote the equality of all people, even ninjas.

9 He won't lash out against those who make fun of the nonbelievers.

10 He will be sympathetic to the scientists, even though they are ruled by reason.

11 He will prove that he is in fact the messiah, but he won't perform miracles to do so.

12 Miracles don't prove much anyway.

13 Hell, David Copperfield made the Statue of Liberty disappear, and he's no messiah.

14 Instead, he will be more like the FSM than any other man.

15 He'll be an amazing prankster and will be pretty damn funny.

16 Contrary to our tradition, he won't even drink beer, will despise strippers and will be a member of a Christian organization.

17 He will even join many Pastafarians together on August 9, 2024 for some kind of silly convention.

Chapter 3

1 "Since we have no real Hell or negative afterlife location, the savior will have nothing to do with saving our souls.

2 But that doesn't mean you get off easy and can be a dick.

3 And you won't be saved just by believing in him and accepting his authority.

4 You gotta do some good deeds too.

5 The messiah will instead help us in this life by protecting us from Darwin's coming enlightenment.

6 Humans by nature use reason.

7 Humans by nature base their knowledge on evidence and logic.

8 We have all been tempted by Darwin and
we have all been tempted to go towards science.

9 Our savior will be so blinded from seeing evidence and reason, so faithful, that he will balance out our unhealthy

logic to save us from the worst of the Apastalypse.

10 He will raise the color pink for all ships and will assemble the dispersed outlaws of the seven seas.

11 He will be the Jolly Roger for all pirates and will unite all Pastafarians as one crew.

12 We will face the coming doom together.

13 Together we will man the cannons of our faith.

14 Together we will hoist our sails to cruise to calmer waters.

15 But sadly, the savior will be persecuted for our beliefs.

16 He will suffer greatly for our asses.

17 He will be made fun of and he will be threatened.

18 He will risk his life at the hands of fanatical nonbelievers and might even get kicked in the balls.

19 And it will be through the Messiah's teachings, his faithfulness, and his suffering, that our Lord Glob, the Flying

Spaghetti Monster, will smite Darwin and his scientific ways.

20 They will bring forth the Kingdom of Pasta and we will finally be rid of evidence and reason."

Chapter 4

1 "Whoa, that sounds pretty sweet," said Steve.

2 "I know dude," replied Captain Jeff, "It'll be awesome.

3 So my brother in FSM, just sit tight for now.

4 Our salvation is near."

Please attend the Pastafarian Convention on August 9, 2024 at Best Western Plus Bradenton Gateway Hotel 2215 Cortez Road W, Bradenton, FL 34207

https://www.facebook.com/PastafarianLooseCanon/

The Book of Solipsy

A testimony

1 For much time did I rest upon my bed in state of revelry and fever, for cold viruses are annoying, and His Holy Cough Medicines do occasionally keep me from sleeping.

2 As I pondered His general tastiness, I thought that perhaps it would be his Holy Meal which would return to me my appetite.

3 Thus, did I prepare The Meal, but of it I could not eat.

4 Instead, I sat and stared into the mass which doth so perfectly represent His Form.

5 How long I sat, I know not, but what filled me were Holy Visions of His Wisdom, and His blessed hopes for the happiness of our lives as His creations and amidst His creations.

6 What follows are the True and Holy Words I was blessed to hear:

7 Thus He Spoke:

8 Begrudge not unto anyone the chosen spirituality that is helpful to them, should it be functional within the real world.

9 My Words shall remind My Creations that, as has been said, there are few atheists on crashing airplanes.

10 Thy life is precious.

11 Desire that yourself and each among you shall have life as long and fun as possible.

12 Hurt no one intentionally, if it can be helped.

13 Be not thou limited by some set of dysfunctional rules in a book that didn't even work 2000 years ago.

14 (Hence all the smiting, crucifying, and such that the book contains.)

15 Update thy thinking to meet with circumstances as they exist around thee.

16 There shall be no shame in it among the intelligent, sayeth I, Who Flies and Is the One True Monster of Steaming Spaghetti.

17 If ye possess any sense at all, it is already known unto you that killing is wrong, stealing is bad, and cheating on ones' espoused love does hurt that person deeply.

18 If ye do these things, ye know it is bad, and should suffer great shame, and should be held accountable.

19 Ye already know this unless ye be dumb as the stone of which is made the mountain.

20 If that is what thee wish to claim, even that shall not be thy defense, though it certainly be true.

21 Thus say I, Whose Appendages Be Noodly and Do Touch.

22 Be good to thine parents should they deserve it, if they did as best they could for you, providing you what they were able and what their resources would allow.

23 Desert them not if in their times of need, and return their kindness, for they are like you, My Creations.

24 If they have beaten you or otherwise been horrible, abusive, interfering jerks who do things to make you miserable, I approve that you may move across the country and out of their presence, and be not even obligated to send them birthday cards.

25 You need only honor them to the degree to which they deserve it, but to that degree you MUST honor them.

26 Should you fail in this, my Noodly Displeasure shall you incur, and you shall be held most shallow and selfish, and shame shall be upon you, say I, Your Tasty and Cheese-Topped One.

27 As for lies, to tell large or illegal falsehoods is most sinful, and those among you with sense already know that.

28 To boast or brag of that which one has not done is most idiotic, and the product of insecurity and childishness.

29 Often the male compelled to tell the boastful lies is the possessor of small intimate parts.

30 If the accursed liar be female, often she is an attention-seeking twit, and you need not abide her company, declare I, Your Extruded and Basil-Garnished One.
31 Small lies, however, maketh the world to turn upon its axis.
32 If ye be dense, I shall clarify: Should ye be asked, for instance, if thine spouses' clothing makes such spouse look fat, ye are to respond with effusive praise of thy loved one's attractiveness and lack of heft, true or not.
33 If thine neighbor should inquire if a gift of cookies were tasty, ye shall reply yea, verily they were most delicious, even though they may have disgusted thee, and ye may have thrown them down the garbage disposer.
34 Should thy aged Grandmother inquire if the Sunday pot roast was pleasing, thou shalt
not reply that it was tough and flavorless, though it were.
35 No!

36 Thou shalt reply that it was a beefy roast unto heaven.

37 Should thy co-worker present thee with a picture of her niece, thou shalt not cry out in horror at the ugliness of the child, for to do so would be rude.

38 Rather, thou must say, verily, what a darling!

39 Art thou catching on, or art thou thick-skulled and dim-witted, ask I, Your Rounded Meaty and Sauced One.

40 As for five other "commandments" with which ye may have familiarity, do as ye will, sayeth the FSM.

41 If some other spirit or power shall catch thy fancy and be of use to thee in time of need, go for it, say I, Your Wise One.

42 Use that spirit not to condemn others, however, for that is among the only times I shall feel compelled to rain down molten sauce upon thee.

43 The Flying Spaghetti Monster will abide no condemnation of His Creatures.

44 If some spirit shall claim that it alone is the one true spirit, and all others will lead to the path of condemnation, then thou shall be mightily suspicious that such a spirit is full of deceit, and THAT spirit is the path of great unhappiness and condemnation.

45 Beware, warn I, of the Semolina and the Tomato.

46 If ye are compelled to draw a picture or sculpt a likeness of that which exists in creation, why on earth is that a bad idea, asks the FSM.

47 To forbid it would be gobbledygook.

48 If thou should like thy neighbor's car better than thine own, and wish to have one as nice, wherein lies the harm?

49 Again, why waste time calling this sin, ask I, Your Noodly and Appendaged One.

50 If ye shall forget occasionally which day of the week it is because thy schedule is overbooked or thou art ill or on vacation, pick some other day to have a Holy Meal of My Offering.

51 Kick back and drink a brewsky.

52 Watch a movie.

53 Relax.

54 I will smite the not for such a silly thing on few occasions.

55 Should thou stub one's toe mightily upon a rock, or lose one's wallet or car keys, or find oneself in some other moment in which thou finds it helpful or humorous to cry out HOLY FLYING SPAGHETTI MONSTER, or FLYING SPAGHETTI MONSTER DAMN IT!!!!, fear not, for I find it kind of funny, and also funny that it shall cause those around thee to look upon thee as if thou art marginally insane.

56 Shout away, say I, Your Glutinous and Whimsically Shaped Lord.

57 That, my True Believers, is the easy stuff.

58 As my Pastafarians, whom I have gathered together and have touched with mine Noodly Appendages, I call upon thee to go beyond ten rules, five of which

are blatantly obvious and five of which are stupid.

59 When thou see people in need – those who have less than thee, those who are ill, those who are young, old, helpless in any way – help them in any way you are able.

60 Even if you are of meager means, share what you have, for that is where many another religion fails.

61 Do better and be examples, instruct I, Your Wiggly Creator of All that is Taught as Science.

62 I, an Invisible Giant Floating Glob of Sauce-Covered Noodles and Round Meat, have no need for your money or resources, BUT, your fellow humans do.

63 I appreciate your love and praise and such, but lots of people right around your immediate vicinity need your love and worldy resources a whole lot more.

64 Don't be so idiotic as to throw your money at people who live in mansions and beseech thee for thy cash, and speak as if endowed with authority from other giant, invisible thingees.

65 Come on, people.

66 Wise up, say I, Your Holy Boiled Grain-Based Nutritious One.

67 If ye have been blessed with great resources, such as to have been born with a silver spoon in your mouth, ye are to remember that it is not thine spit which hath coated that spoon with silver.

68 Thou should be especially grateful for thy blessings, and especially giving of thy resources.

69 Ye will not be taking it with you into the Stripper Factory, nor need it at the Beer Volcano.

70 Money is only good for the good it can do the living.

71 Quit being so greedy, for greed is vile unto me and unto your fellow Creations, say I, Your Well-Seasoned Al dente One.

72 Be active in your government, and stand against those things which are unfair and make no sense.

73 Be civil in your disagreements for they shall always be with thee, and

rational in your debates, for ye shall always have them.

74 Do you really need a Giant Glob of Noodles, Sauce, and Meat to tell you this?

75 Do you really need to drink the transubstantiated blood of some historical personage to make you feel superior?

76 The Flying Spaghetti Monster is a little freaked out by that, frankly.

77 Get a grip, instruct I, Your Wise and Floating Saucy Monster.

78 Ye have been born, ye are alive, and ye shall die.

79 It's the "ye are alive" part that should concern ye most at the moment.

80 Yes, the Beer Volcano and Stripper Factory of Heaven await thee, and are currently under construction, but ye shall not be so gullible as to count on what ye as yet have no evidence to support.

81 Well, that is how I wish ye would think, anyway.

82 But, since ye apparently aren't quite there yet, if Intelligent Design is to be considered Science, then since every

word of My Great Creation of the
Universe is True, it shall thusly be
considered Science, and thusly taught as
well.

83 Proclaim I, Your Wondrous Glob in
Heaven.

84 And finally, when bad things doth
befall ye as they will, ye are constantly
carping "why me, what did I do to
deserve it, why, why, why???"

85 My Noodlyness heareth not ye bother
to ask such when good things doth befall
ye.

86 Yet, the question is just as valid, and
the answer is the same.

87 Ponder that as ye partake of mine holy
meal.

88 And then did I return from my fevered
revelry, to find my flattened butt still in
my kitchen chair, with a cold plate of His
Holy Meal in front of me, and a paper
inscribed with his inspired words, and a
ball-point pen run out of ink.

89 I rushed to my microwave and
reheated my meal, for it was a miracle!

90 My appetite had returned, and I did eat, and praise Him, and return to my bed and fall to a deep slumber.

91 In the morning, I re-read His Holy Words, and did check them for typos and misspellings.

92 Truly I am humbled.

93 Truly, by His Wisdom, we are blessed!

94 All Praise the Flying Spaghetti Monster.

Please attend the Pastafarian Convention on August 9, 2024 at Best Western Plus Bradenton Gateway Hotel 2215 Cortez Road W, Bradenton, FL 34207

https://www.facebook.com/PastafarianLooseCanon/

Spaghetti Issues

Below is information about the five main characters:

God: Little is known about God's birth, His parents, His childhood or His origin. We know that He is a flying spaghetti monster that lived a blissful life as a slave. He was banished to a great void and was given almost an unlimited creative ability but refrained from using those powers for 8 years. During those 8 years He lived in a fruitless state of self pity while being continually comforted by the voice of his mother. On August 9, 1613 the voice of God's mother stopped. On that day God created the universe that we have learned to enjoy even to this day. He is normally uninvolved with the affairs of man but does operate behind the scenes in ways that He doesn't want anybody to know. At sometime during 2005 God met with a 13 year old girl named Ashley. God attempted to transport Ashley to the beginning of His life but failed in His efforts. On Ashley's 21st birthday God visited her a second time to teach her all of the wisdom that was needed to live as a servant of God. The values of dedication, silence, submission, humility, dishonesty and hypocrisy are to be known to the entire world. God chose Ashley to teach these concepts to all mankind.

Ashley: Ashley was born in Century, Florida on December 25, 1991. She grew up in a Baptist church in a very dedicated Baptist family. Her devotion to God was obvious to everyone in her life. Her charismatic personality and her sincere spirit made her a fine Christian girl with a potential to do great things for God.

Everyone loved her and treated her like a hero even though she had never done anything heroic. That changed when she met God face to face as a 13 year old girl. She became even more devoted to God and more of an inspirational hero to those around her. The only difference was that before meeting God she believed in her faith. After meeting God she became a skeptic of the Christian religion but never shared that fact for the remainder of her life. Ashley suffers with a multitude of moral failings after meeting God the second time. During this period of moral, financial, social, emotional and relational failings she learns all that she needs to know to be a servant of God. Ashley is the first person to live her life as a servant of God. This did not hinder her from being actively involved in the Southern Baptist community. Ashley is quoted as saying, "True Servants of God are to live in secret until our official church is established in the latter days. The Church of God of Latter Day Fakes will be established on August 9, 2413 on the 800th anniversary of the earth." Ashley was chosen to find the history of God's life but instead ended up writing God's future with the famous book titled, "Spaghetti Issues".

Mary: Mary was born October 31, 1957. She is Ashley's maternal grandmother. At age 43 Mary married someone of the Mormon faith and left behind the Baptist tradition. Mary was fascinated by the Mormon Church, their teachings, their energy and their pro-family position. Even though Mary wasn't disowned by her family she slowly drifted away because of the obvious tension that existed because of her religious choices. Mary's relationship to Ashley, her mother and her sisters never diminished. Her bond was obviously strongest to Ashley's oldest sister. Many believe that Mary paid for Ashley's oldest sister's college, her car and her home upon completing college but Mary always denied it. Mary had a fascination with Halloween and always dressed as a Pirate on Halloween and handed out candy to children. It was even rumored that Mary gave small sums of money to single mothers on that day. Mary always denied it. During Ashley's eight year journey of moral failing Mary came to visit Ashley every single Halloween and gave her a sum of money sufficient to help her through the year but never gave her too much. This is the only act of generosity that Mary ever admitted. Even her mandatory tithes to the Mormon Church were given with cash. Mary was reprimanded the first five years that she belonged to the Mormon Church for failing to give her tithes. She denied the false accusations but promised to forgive them for bearing false witness against her. She assured them that their lack of records did not equate to moral failure on her part. Ashley even believed that her grandmother was a true servant of God but never asked her and had no intentions of doing so. Mary was the only person of comfort to Ashley during her days of moral failing.

Edna - Edna was born in Century, Florida sometime during the year 1891, 1892 or 1893. In August of 1913 Edna began fasting. Fasting in excess of 5 days causes the body to emit an odor that grabs the attention of God. It is a pleasant aroma that always pleases God but Edna's odor began to intensify which placed God in an extended state of ecstasy. God began to scrutinize Edna's past and discovered a most benevolent, selfless and devoted creature. Unfortunately Edna was a paranoid skeptic unwilling to do the work of God.

Satan - Satan is the only male character mentioned in Spaghetti Issues. This is later remedied by his requirement to behave as a female while wearing lipstick and a dress. Satan was an ambitious plant that attempted to take God's throne but failed. God was impressed with his ambition and used it against him. Satan spends the remainder of his life carrying out the tasks that God hates to do. Even though he is a miserable slave it is suspected that he is constantly planning and plotting for the perfect opportunity to overthrow God.

Chapter 1 - The Goal of This Book

The goal of this book is to protect the strength of established religions while encouraging an open mind to its followers. The need will arise in the future for a superior deity. True Servants of God will lead the way in this effort because of the advantage gained by centuries of submission to established custom without the disadvantage of the resignation of the mind. Get on board now by enthusiastically joining your local church, mosque, synagogue, parish, temple or other trustworthy institution. Become involved with the tradition to which you are most familiar. This will reduce your level of social discomfort but most importantly this is the environment God has provided for you. Do not rebel against it.

There are analogical equivalents of God in your life. This can cause your faith to become weaker or stronger. Changing jobs, a change in management, a new landlord, new relationship, loss of relationship, purchase of a home, starting a business, changes in government leadership or any other changes in perceived hierarchy within your environment can alter your understanding of God. This does not offend God unless your disrespect for Him becomes obvious with your tone. You should always remain committed to God in a consistent manner without regard to the condition of your hopelessly fickle mind. If you choose to believe God does not exist, your trust for authority figures diminishes to an illogical level. You will begin to carry an unreasonable burden upon your own shoulders. Your resentment, disregard and/or disrespect for God will be thrust upon undeserving nurturers in your life. These nurturers may or may not respond to your attacks with benevolence. These nurturers are likely to respond in a way to destroy you with unforgiving hatred. If you choose to believe in God, respect Him and trust Him with your every need, then your relationship with authority will be pleasant and rewarding. You will carry a light burden which is precisely your duty. Be aware of your tendency to correlate God's character with the character of the authorities that you presently experience.

The consequences of unbelief should be carefully considered. You should never choose to prefer logic which is certain to destroy any good idea. Logic can prove everything therefore it proves nothing. Be aware of the outcomes of specific ideas. Embrace the ideas that are beneficial. Discard the ideas that are destructive. You should embrace the beneficial ideas because they are beneficial. You should reject those ideas that are destructive because they are destructive. Logic is a worthless substitute for thinking.

Chapter 1 - Non-existent chapter

None of the contents of this chapter shall ever be proclaimed publicly. If you are reading this book for entertainment or educational purposes, these principles can be applied to your religious or work life. There is one essential ingredient for all levels of leadership and servant hood. Honesty is a virtue that should never be applied within an organization. Honesty is reserved for intimate friendships and family relations. Honesty is a noble characteristic of an individual but it can be destructive within a business, government or religious institution. All servants of God must deny the contents of this chapter and even the existence of this chapter.

Hypocrisy is the highest virtue of the servants of God.

Truth is unattainable. Truth is inaccessible.

Certain elements of our environment do provide certainty. A tree is a tree and does possess the qualities of a tree. There could be negative consequences associated with ignoring or disbelieving this physical truth.

Intangible truth such as history, science, astronomy and the like can be ignored without negative consequences. The belief that Abraham Lincoln was the 16th president can be doubted without ill outcome resulting to the unbeliever.

Truth is an obsession that creates many a fool. Intangible truths do not hold any value other than satisfying the curiosity of an individual. Fictitious stories can easily replace intangible truth. If a fictitious story has superior value it should be preferred to the intangible and unknown truth. Intangible truths are always unknown to the masses. In cases of history or religion the truth is unknown to all. Claiming something to be true gives power to the spokesman. This persuasive encounter produces believers who proclaim the received information to be true. This pandemic obsession with the word truth causes great abuse to the word itself. A claim can be proven to such a small group of people that it still has the qualities of being unproven. Faith is still required by the average individual. The most persuasive story prevails.

Eventually the most socially acceptable story prevails and receives a societal stamp as truth. This stamp of truth does not validate the fact(s). Most fact(s) will never be validated. Aside from physical truth, truth is unattainable and inaccessible. Embrace the superior idea regardless of its status as truth. End the truth obsession and believe in the beneficial. The Bible is one example of a beneficial substitute for truth. Other beneficial substitutes have been in circulation since God created the universe on August 9, 1613 and these substitutes have repeatedly been proven to be beneficial to the adherent.

The depth required to uncover realities is unreachable. The quest for truth is one of disappointment and folly. A seemingly true system is sufficient for eternal happiness. Proven systems are in existence to supply eternal peace and abundant wisdom. Because of flawed logic based upon involuntarily adopted philosophies these systems cannot be wholeheartedly followed. However culture has always existed. Several religions have survived these fluctuations in the level of devotion of its adherents.

It is certain that devotion can be developed through hypocrisy. Don't let the purist demands of religion cause you to abandon such a valuable resource.

Our thoughts sway from day to day. We hear a new idea. The idea may sound awesome even though it contradicts an idea that we have held dear for decades. The human mind is so fickle that we believe anything that is disguised with logic. A man that holds firm to a set of principles is noble even if he doesn't believe those principles on that particular day. Maybe he believes something that is very destructive but promotes an idea that is beneficial to him and mankind as a whole. Hypocrisy is not a shameful thing. The foolish quest for truth is much more shameful and a massive waste of time.

Some people teach us that nothing matters at all. They tell us that ethics are only important to the extent that we enjoy following them. Even though this is very appealing and logical it is easy to recognize that this thought process provides no value at all. It cannot possibly improve anyone's life to spread such a depressing message. It is better to keep this destructive idea a secret and follow something loftier even if the competing idea is less appealing and illogical. Don't be a fool just to enjoy the luxury of being right all the time. Use beneficial philosophies for the benefit of us all.

It has been said that we cannot impose our spirituality on anyone anymore than anyone else. This is completely false. The purpose of a philosopher is to install the "truth" into the minds of as many people as possible without being detected. We have many values that were imposed upon us. To shed those ideas would require years of effort and retraining. We should all be philosophers and force society to think in a more beneficial way. The fruitful philosopher can do this without being detected and is probably someone that will never be classified as a philosopher. Make the world better by making the brains of mankind better.

Nobody in history has ever uncovered a perfect ideology. Almost all philosophies result in survival of the adherent. Every argument has a counter argument. If both debaters have equivalent skill at debating, the argument and counter argument will be equal. It is preferable to see someone stand firm whether they are being honest or not. Otherwise he appears a fool and will not be trusted by anyone. A skilled debater will try to trick their opponent into making a fool out of himself. It is more advantageous to sabotage the credibility of your opponent than to make a superior argument. Your advantage becomes greater if you can convince your opponent to sabotage himself. Your character and your image are the most effective tools that you have. If you are respected, your ideas will be adopted by those who are uninterested in philosophy. Do not focus on uncovering a superior idea. Such an idea does not exist or it would have already been revealed. It is more important that you focus on portraying yourself as superior by embracing a set of principles. That is your greatest obstacle and your most powerful tool.

Chapter 2 - Creation from God's Perspective

The earliest memory that God had was living in a happy town with His sisters and His mother. One day His mother became angry because He changed His sauce into many flavors. His mother cried with shame. She said that alfredo sauce is not fit for any flying spaghetti monster. God was concerned for His fate because He knew that His mother was cruel. God's mother told him that He could no longer live in the happy town of joyful slaves. God was sentenced to be a ruler of the highest order. Instantly He was transported into a great void. His mother's voice rang loudly within this void for 8 years. God heard these words, "You are a perfect being with all your noodliness. You can create any creature that your imagination can ponder but none can be perfect. All of your creation must be flawed in some way. The Flying Spaghetti Monster is the only perfect being." These words of His mother rang loudly into His meatballs, caused His sauce to stir and made His noodles to quiver. It was soothing to hear the voice of His mother but at the end of 8 years her voice stopped. God cried, yelled and tried to gain His mother's attention. God became angry with His mother and that is when the creation began.

On the first day God created a mountain, a tree and a midget to serve as a curse upon His mother. He could not remember why His mother hated these things but somehow He knew that she did. This did not gain the attention of His mother so He created a sky with a heaven. The heaven was full of beer volcanoes and stripper factories. He became tired and hit the beer volcano pretty hard. On the next day while still drunk He completed creation. It was a great day. God created 428,713,300 humans on that day. The humans were made in the image of the midget only larger. God deeply desired to create a race of Flying Spaghetti Monsters but was not able. He remembered the words of His mother. "All of your creation must be flawed in some way. The flying spaghetti monster is the only perfect being." God looked upon His creation and realized that He did ok. He was impaired by His beer consumption and also limited with His inability to create other flying spaghetti monsters. This day was marked as August 9, 1613. Just for fun He gave humans the illusion that the earth was 1613 years older than it actually was. He was interested in how the humans would fill in the history of the past 1613 years because they were very curious and mischievous creatures. Most of them were prone to lie profusely to gain advantage one over another. The humans were all programmed never to seek beyond January 1, 0 because He had caused this to appear to be the beginning of time. God knew that if their imaginations reached beyond that date that He could no longer control these humans. There had to be limits. Without limits God has no control and humans have no peace.

Chapter 3 - Exhaustion of Being God

In 1813 God became exhausted with His duties of being an omnipotent deity. He decided to rest for a few years and live as an olive tree but someone was needed to rule over the earth in His absence. The olive tree was unwilling to take His place. The olive tree said that her life was good as an olive tree. She was well respected, wealthy and had more than she could ever need. She thought it would be foolish to give all of that up just to be ruler of the whole world. Then God decided to approach the grape vine. The grape vine was less gracious and responded rather violently. The grape vine said unto Him, "I have lived my life by a set of principles. I seek every opportunity to bring joy to others. I produce delicious grapes, hardy raisins and exquisite wines with my fruit. The joy I experience by seeing the joy of others is something I could never give away. I would certainly not trade it for an opportunity to bully people around and force them to do the things that I want them to do. That life bears intense pain, unbearable rejection and emptiness beyond measure. Get away from me. Go talk to Satan."

Before God had a chance to seek out another plant to take His place He was approached by Satan who quickly accepted His offer, crowned himself King and began speaking of his plans to restructure the planet. He was a beautiful vine, an eloquent speaker, bore the most delicious fruit but his ambition was unsettling. All the other plants catered to him and praised him publicly. When the plants spoke among themselves they discussed their fear and hatred for Satan. God began to second guess His decision to make him ruler of the world but it was already a done deal. God was confused. He had not yet become Satan. Was this another limitation that was imposed upon Him by His mother? God began discussing His predicament with the fig tree. The fig tree told Him that if He had honestly chosen Satan to take His place then He should rejoice and celebrate His time of rest as a Satan. If you didn't chose him, if you were somehow coerced by use of force, manipulation, trickery, bribery or deceit then we will all suffer and he will be destroyed along with us. God soon realized that Satan had deceived Him with his slick talk and his ambitious forcefulness. Satan began to argue with God when God reminded him that there was never an agreement to trade positions. Satan demanded that God tell him to whom He had been speaking. God did not want to tell him. God insisted to speak to the highest authority to protect Him from this unruly and belligerent plant. Sadly, God is the highest authority. This fight belonged to Him. This arguing and intimidation exhausted Him greatly and He needed something to eat. He searched the fig tree for food but He found nothing but leaves. This caused Him to experience intense anger. He cursed the fig tree and said, "Nobody shall ever eat of your fruit forever. If I can't have your sweet goodness, nobody can." With these words the fig tree was burned to the ground with fire. God began to eat from the fruit of Satan until his fruit was no more. God divided Satan into many types of plants and called him thistles, weeds, brambles and briars. God soon recognized that thistles, weeds, brambles and briars could destroy all of the plants that He had met with disapproval. In exchange for Satan's new found power he was forbidden from telling anyone that he was a male. He was required to be feminine in all his ways but was obligated to destroy those plants who failed God with the heartless violence of a male. Many animals, humans and former plants hated thistles, weeds, brambles and briars. They called him a sissy. Thistles, weeds, brambles and briars always responded with much eloquence and grace. He proclaimed that he would always protect the plants and do what is best for everybody involved. He appeared not to be phased by the words of these animals, humans and former plants. Then thistles, weeds, brambles and briars would plead to God that the harshest and swiftest violence be imposed upon those who challenged his wickedness. God always agreed to carry out the demands of thistles, weeds, brambles and briars but in reality God never done anything about it.

He just enjoyed watching him get so defeated time after time. He could have been destroyed as the fig tree but instead God was able to torture thistle, weeds, bramble and briars for eternity. God was so entertained by this ongoing relationship. He maintained His role as God but He no longer had the hassle of doing all of the dirty work in His kingdom. Thistles, weeds, brambles and briars remained His slave forever. He had to do all of His dirty work but had to wear a dress and lipstick the whole time.

In 1913 God tried again to take a rest from His duties. This time He decided to approach a young woman by the name of Edna. Edna lived her life with such compassion for her fellow humans as well as the beasts and plants. God lifted Edna up high and placed her upon a mountain that allowed her to see all the lands of the earth. God told Edna that she could have dominion over all the earth for a period of 70 years if she would just acknowledge that He was the ruler of the whole world. Edna had just been engaging in a spiritual experiment. She had not eaten any food in 12 days. She thought God was playing some trick on her and was trying to exploit her physical weakness. She said, "Am I supposed to believe that a flying spaghetti monster is the ruler of the world? Surely you seek to withdraw a humorous reaction from me. Take me off of this mountain at once." God did not wish to hold Edna against her will but Edna was the only human fit to take God's place. God politely placed Edna back inside of her home. Edna spent the next three days praying and feasting upon spaghetti with a side of garlic bread. Edna did not want to rule the earth. God's vacation plans would be delayed another

100 years. The next time God sought a vacation He decided to give himself an extra 8 years to prepare. In 2005 God found the precious Ashley and prepared her to establish her reign as manager of the world. Ashley needed to understand paradox. God needed her to believe in doubt. Ashley needed to be devoted to hypocrisy. God needed Ashley to be dishonest about her honesty. He needed Ashley to understand her inability to understand. He needed Ashley to remain loyal while having an open mind. God contradicts himself frequently. He doesn't need someone who questions His inconsistencies. He doesn't need someone to attack Him with the phrase, "but you said." He doesn't need someone that will speak their mind. Paradox is beautiful. Paradox is powerful. Paradox is everywhere. Good people hate paradox. God needs evil followers with a

capacity to do that which is good. God despises good followers who only have the capacity to act with great wickedness. It is better to be evil than to be good. This allows you the flexibility to choose either. Being good isn't appropriate for every situation. Do not use your status as evil to indulge yourself. Use it only as a license to expand your arsenal of weapons. Prefer good. Embrace that which is good. Never categorize yourself as good. This severely limits your capacity to survive and sabotages your moral character.

Those who commit evil acts never do so with the intention of being evil. Those who commit evil always behave that way because they believe it is good. Good is the only cause of evil. Stop trying to be good. This will cause you to fail morally. Be evil. It is on the only way to be good.

Catastrophic evil is always committed by those that are doing the right thing. Those who embrace their sinful nature never cause catastrophic evil.

Chapter 4 - Creation Re-experienced through Ashley

Ashley approached her window in the early morning to pray unto her Lord and Saviour Jesus Christ. Her mood that day was especially peaceful and submissive. She didn't normally arise this early. It was almost as if she had been awoken gently by a small child in a playful mood. To arise this early in such a pleasant state of mind reminded her of her Lord and Saviour Jesus Christ that was always with her. She was overwhelmed with his presence and majesty. He seemed so close. Ashley looked out her window. A mass of spaghetti with two eyes lay in a field outside of her window. Without any effort, Ashley quickly leapt out of her window. Before she fell to the ground this mass of spaghetti reached out to break her fall. The mass of spaghetti spoke unto Ashley. "I am God. You have been chosen to go to the time of my birth to explore my origins." Ashley was launched into a capsule of time with God's longest noodle. Ashley saw before her four flying spaghetti monsters. Three of them were covered with tomato based sauce. The one appeared to be God. His image was very similar to the other three flying spaghetti monsters with the exception of His alfredo sauce. The largest flying spaghetti monster of the four became angry and began beating the flying spaghetti monster covered with alfredo sauce. She told him that she hated him and would never see him again. She spoke of a deceptive midget who lived under a tree on top of a mountain. The largest flying spaghetti monster said unto God, "I will kill that tree and that midget right before I crush that mountain so that your sisters may never change their sauce. I hate you so much. Go away! Go away! Go away!" Even though Ashley was in the presence of such hostilities she continued to remain in a peaceful and submissive state. Ashley closed her eyes to imagine what it might have been like to feel such hostility from her own mother. When Ashley re-opened her eyes she witnessed a great nothingness. It was dark as night but she could see for millions of miles. As far as she could see there was nothing, nothing and more nothing. She looked down at her hands but they were noodles. Without the assistance of a mirror Ashley was able to examine her whole body. She was God. No longer did she feel at peace. She became full of sorrow, rage and euphoria because she knew that she had great powers. Ashley wanted to use all of her power to punish the larger spaghetti monster which she saw beating God in her previous vision. She could not. In a fit of rage she created a mountain, a tree and a midget. This left her feeling disappointed and foolish for her rash behavior. She continued to create a sky with a heaven. The heaven contained a beer volcano and a stripper factory. Ashley wanted to sip the beer from the beer volcano. As a thirteen year old girl she knew this was not allowed. Ashley closed her eyes again because she was trying to fight the urge to drink from the beer volcano. When she re-opened her eyes she was back in her room staring out her window. She made eye contact with God but neither of them spoke. They continued to maintain eye contact for several hours. They remained in continuous silence. Ashley's mother entered the room and told her it was time for dinner. Ashley had missed the entire day. It was now 7:08pm. She was puzzled as to how her absence for the day was entirely unnoticed by her mother and her two sisters. Ashley was starved more than any point in her life to which she had any memory. She began eating her dinner without saying a prayer. Ashley's mother stared at her in disbelief because Ashley was always insistent that the family pray before meals. Once Ashley finished eating her spaghetti she had a great desire to have a beer. She quickly walked to the refrigerator and began frantically searching for beer. Her mother noticed her frustration and asked what she was trying to find. Ashely said, "I cannot find the beer." Ashley's sisters began to laugh hysterically. She was not joking but she immediately realized her sisters' laughter was justified. It was against Baptist custom to consume alcoholic beverages. Ashley became so embarrassed by her slip of the tongue but more so she was confused at why she had the desire to drink beer. Ashley said, "I was only joking." She then grabbed a bottle of water out of the refrigerator. Ashley's sense of morality had somehow vanished. She ate without saying a prayer, she was willing to consume beer, and she lied and even ate food made in the image of the creator of the universe. Ashley knew that she had been touched by God's noodley appendage but what did this mean for her future?

Chapter 5 - Hope

For many years Ashley remembered that moment. She would look out her window often hoping that God would appear unto her again. Ashley firmly believed that God would come again. Even though Ashley knew that Christianity was false she had become even more dedicated to her faith. She followed all Christian/Baptist traditions and studied the Bible with more frequency and intensity. Her faith was weaker than ever. In all fairness, her faith was less than weak, it was non-existent. The fear of disappointing others, the guilt of being incapable to live up to the standards set forth in her faith and the confusion of not knowing what Jesus wanted her to do was completely gone. Hypocrisy is an accusation that is often directed toward Christians. It is a badge of shame that none of them ever want to wear. Ashley was now a hypocrite because she no longer believed in the traditions and teachings of Christianity. Oddly, she was not ashamed. Her hypocrisy was a secret that she would never share with anyone. Ashley believed she would continue to be showered with respect from people on the inside and the outside of her faith. Ashley's passion, enthusiasm, discipline, patience and joy by far exceeded that of anybody currently living at that time. Ashley had certainly been touched by God's noodley appendage but what did this mean for her future? She patiently waited and confidently expected the second coming of God.

Ashley graduated from high school. She left for college. She had still not seen God. Every time she visited home she would look out her window awaiting God's second coming. On Vasudera's 21st birthday December 25, 2012 she was visiting her home during the period of Holiday. That is when God did come a second time. This time God visited

Ashley in the night. God said unto Ashley, "All the stores are closed but tomorrow you must go buy beer. You are of legal age and mental maturity. Your life is about to change for the worse. Stick with me and adhere to all my teachings. I will make you the greatest hypocrite and phony of all time. Buy the beer and I will see you tomorrow. You will even learn the highest virtue of my servants." Ashley wanted to speak. She wanted to argue. She wanted to ask questions. The request that God made didn't make any sense. It seemed wrong. It seemed stupid. Ashley didn't know how she was going to be able to pull it off. Ashley was completely pissed off and confused. Somehow without planning for this moment she knew the right thing to do was to pretend it was a great idea, smile and say, "Yes sir." Ashley was able to smile but she was unable to speak. Ashley feared that her insincerity would be noticed by God. She was afraid God would see through her flattering words used to confirm her half hearted submission. It worked out better that Ashley became temporarily mute. Ashley's insincerity might have been detected in her voice and put God in a state of rage.

That night Ashley had trouble sleeping. She fantasized about hateful things that she should have said to God. She even fantasized about chopping off His noodles and kicking Him hard in the meatballs. Ashley screamed out loud, "What a dick! I never drink beer. Why am I supposed to get excited about my life getting worse? Maybe I am taking this all wrong. Perhaps I am mentally ill and seeing visions that really aren't there. How stupid is it that a flying spaghetti monster created the universe?" The more she said, "A flying spaghetti monster created the universe," the stupider she felt about the situation. Ashley did not want to buy beer. She did not want to meet with God again. It was fortunate that Ashley did not have a rebellious spirit. She eventually settled down and remembered something very important. The best thing to do when you are faced with an undesirable task is to pretend to enjoy it. She was asleep within moments after reminding herself of this very effective technique. She quietly spoke to herself the following words, "It will be fine. It is a joy to buy beer. It is a joy to be the servant of a flying spaghetti monster."

Chapter 6 - The Holy Task

Ashley slept late into the afternoon. Whenever she awoke her sister was there

with her. Everyone else was gone.
Ashley's sister asked her for a ride to the
movie theatre. This annoyed Ashley
because she had to buy beer and couldn't
do it in front of her sister. Ashley smiled
and told her sister that it was no big deal.
Ashley took her sister to the movie
theatre but she knew she would have to
pick her up again in a few hours. She
would be unable to buy the beer until
afterwards. She went to a nearby mall
and began to walk furiously throughout
the stores. She was unable to take her
mind off of the fact that her sister and
God were out to destroy her day. To
make matters worse Ashley ran into her
grandmother at the mall who wanted her
to come over with her sister for a late
dinner. Ashley was on fire. She was
consumed with an anger that
overwhelmed her. She wanted to scream
and punch anything within her reach but

she restrained herself because she was in public after all. Ashley told her grandmother that it was no big deal. Ashley's mother and her other sister soon found out about dinner at their grandmother's house. They all met there. Ashley got there around 7pm. Her grandmother had not started cooking. Ashley was pissed off and hungry. Being hungry, spending the last several hours in rage and having just five hours to accomplish a task that she still had no idea how it would be achieved caused Ashley great anguish. It was almost unbearable. She wanted to scream and kick. She was going completely insane. Around 8:30 they began to eat lemon pepper chicken with green beans and mashed potatoes. It was a simple meal but one that Ashley was grateful to finally have the pleasure of eating. Everyone looked at Ashley as usual. She was always the one expected to say a prayer over the food because of the emotion and power in which she always prayed. This is something she usually did with joy. Ashley was well aware that her prayers were a source of inspiration and emotional entertainment to all who knew her. In the moment of hunger, rage and a nagging anxiety she was still able to pull off an A+ prayer. This was evident to Ashley because she seen the tears streaming down the face of her oldest sister. Ashley was unmoved emotionally by her performance. This was unusual but this was not a normal day. The chicken was wonderful. Everything was delicious. The food gave her a moment's relief from the anxiety that she had been experiencing the whole day but it quickly came back when the food was consumed. It was now 9:30. Ashley had no idea how she was going to buy beer without being seen by any of her family. Luckily her mother and her sisters all left together. This allowed Ashley to drive home alone but the reason they left her there was to catch up with her grandmother.

The night unfolded into a most unusual event. Ashley was fidgeting nervously because she knew that she had a sacred task to complete before midnight. Her grandmother was gone for twenty minutes which just increased her anxiety and anger. Normally Ashley and her grandmother stayed up together talking for hours. Her grandmother was pre occupied with something other than having heart to heart discussions with Ashley.

"Ashley," her grandmother called in a most unusual accent. "Ashley," she called a second time in the same accent. "Oh Ashley," she called once more. It was obvious to Ashley that her grandmother was being playful. It reminded Ashley of her childhood. Ashley was expecting her grandmother to come out in her pirate's costume like she did when Ashley was a child. Out she popped in full pirate costume including the eye patch. Her grandmother blurted out loudly, "We're out to get some grog." She handed Ashley a handful of jolly ranchers. Ashley was greatly confused but gleeful because of the pleasant childhood memories that were subconsciously being thrust upon her. "Where are we going?" Ashley asked. "Nowhere! Not with you dressed like that." her grandmother shouted. She handed Ashley an eye patch and pointed at a pirate's costume. Ashley laughed and pleaded, "I am not a kid anymore. It isn't Halloween and we are going out in public." Logically this seemed to be a foolish thing to do but

Ashley was experiencing a childlike euphoria. She went along with it. She was excited about where things were headed. Ashley said, "Yes ma'am" in a very reluctant tone. It was very odd. Every part of the costume fit Ashley perfectly. It was almost as if her grandmother had this whole thing planned. Ashley's imagination was running in circles. What did her grandmother have up her sleeve? "Arghh! Let's go! Let's go! Ahoy matey!" her grandmother said in an angry tone. For the second time Ashley asked her grandmother where they were going. Her grandmother said, "Ashley dear, you are twenty one years old. You are of legal age and mental maturity. It's time for you to start living like a pirate. We are going to buy beer. Of course! What else did you have planned for tonight?" Ashley's grandmother was a devout

Mormon that never drank beer. Ashley became confused, embarrassed and relieved all at the same time. The orders that she had received from God were falling into place. When they arrived together at the gas station Ashley did not wait for her grandmother. She boldly entered the store to purchase a six pack of beer and quickly walked to the car. She was full of courage to complete a holy task but also anxious to get back to the car. Her grandmother was just as anxious. She did the same thing. They were not at the gas station very long at all. The whole drive back was completely silent other than the blowing of the heater in the car. Neither of them spoke at all. Ashley was thinking to herself, "Wow! I have just finished the most holy task of my life. It is the first time I have ever performed a direct order from any god. It doesn't feel exciting. It doesn't feel peaceful. I am not happy about it. In fact I'm pretty sick. I feel like I've been swindled, cheated, abused and manipulated. I have just been beaten and outsmarted. I am very humiliated and my grandmother seen the whole thing. This just intensifies the humiliation." When they arrived at her grandmother's house her grandmother began crying audibly but not too loud. She opened the beer one bottle at a time and poured it down the drain. Ashley followed suit and did the same thing. When the beer had all been poured out her grandmother hugged Ashley for several minutes and apologized to her. Her grandmother said, "I don't know what came over me. I was excited about your birthday and I wanted to do something memorable with you. I have never drank beer in my life and that has worked well for me. I should have never attempted to corrupt you." Ashley began crying as well. Ashley felt just as humiliated as her grandmother did but at the same time her grandmother's actions were a life saver. Ashley didn't dare tell her grandmother about her experiences with the Flying Spaghetti Monster. That was a secret that she would never tell anybody. Ashley assured her grandmother that all was well and reminded her that this was a very memorable birthday. Ashley changed back into her normal clothes and went back home for the night. She slept well for the next several nights until it was time for her to return back to college. Nothing unusual happened. Ashley did not see God. She did not speak to her grandmother for the remainder of her time at home. She wasn't exactly eager to go back to college but there were a few people that she was looking forward to seeing again. Her holy task was completed yet she was filled with embarrassment, guilt and shame. Is this what it feels like to serve God?

Chapter 7 - Second Holy Task

Several months had passed since Ashley had followed God's instructions to purchase beer. God intentionally assigned a senseless task without purpose or reason just to test Ashley's faith. He had to test her to see if her attitude gave her the capacity to be molded and shaped into something wonderful. Ashley was a perfect candidate to spread Ashley's message throughout the world so that God could take a blessed vacation. Ashley already knew that the best thing to do when faced with an undesirable task was to pretend to enjoy it. This is the essence of hypocrisy and insincerity. Ashley was approached while in her dorm room. God said to her, "Ashley, I have something that I need you to understand but do you trust me to show you the way?" Ashley responded, "I do trust you yet I have my doubts about the pleasure of the task you have for me to do. Will I be jumping on top of dogs or chopping off the left leg of a possum?" God swiftly struck Ashley to the ground with a quick kick and the sound of blasting thunder. God demanded that Ashley speak to Him with respect. Ashley stood up with her head held high and said, "Yes my blessed God. I know you will show me the way."

God began to speak and said, "I need you to take a handful of salt packets from the college cafeteria. I want you to eat two of them at a time and drink as much water as you desire. Repeat this process until you have finished all of them." Ashley began the process of consuming the salt which was created, buried in the earth and scattered throughout the oceans. The precious mineral that God loved more than any of His creation was now becoming a part of Ashley. Ashley took the salt and even displayed a childlike smile while doing so. Later on she began to lose her complexion and slowed down her process. She became ill and began to vomit. God commanded her to stop and told her that too much salt is not good for anyone.

"Salt is intended to bring flavor to the blandest of food such as the white of an egg. Salt is intended to preserve that which quickly decays. Salt even preserves the vastness of the oceans which hold this world together. Salt is not intended to build houses. Salt is not intended to build nations. Salt is not intended to be consumed in mass quantities. When salt becomes weak it is good for nothing. Extreme viewpoints, extreme religions, extreme philosophies and extreme political ideologies are of great importance. They are the salt of the earth. If they ever compromise their values the ocean will dry up and the world will collapse. You must protect these powerful institutions and ensure that their influence is not destroyed. You, Ashley are not the salt. You are food that provides substance to the people. They must eat your words to maintain their sanity when the salt becomes too strong. Too much salt can destroy your well being. A shortage of salt will collapse the world. Salt cannot stand on its own. I once turned a woman into a pile of salt. I intended to turn her into a pillar of salt but the salt collapsed. Salt cannot stand on its own. I love salt more than any of my creation. I love salt more than I love you. My favorite humans are those who are the salt. I even like them more than you. The salt causes you to vomit. The salt causes womankind to become stronger. Please do not allow them to perish. When they began to doubt or feel like fools I want you to be there to feed them with reality. The salt will make them sick and cause them to vomit. It will cause them to abandon their faith or their silly organizations. Give them a bowl of spaghetti, a shot of sweet tea and equip them with my words. That is your duty as my servant. Serve Me and ensure that my shelves are always stocked with salt."

Chapter 8 - Nature of God

God continued to speak to Ashley. There was still much for Ashley to learn. God began to speak,

"I am eager to teach you the hard lessons of life but I do understand that the nature of my existence is curious to you. Let's get this out of the way to avoid the delay of teaching you the important lessons of life. Every effect must first have a cause. This means all effects can be traced back to a previous cause. This is an art that humans find entertaining. This is why so much history exists. I created the universe on August 9, 1613 but you notice much history exists before that date. People love to find an origin to an origin and then find that origin's origin. It appears to be an infinite process but any fool knows there has to be an original cause. One exception applies to that rule. Even a child knows that spaghetti is so wonderful that no reason is needed to enjoy spaghetti. At first I was only spaghetti. Flying came natural to me and my uncanny existence caused me to define myself as a monster. I am a Flying Spaghetti Monster that was forced to rule the universe as a punishment from my mother. My mother was a traditionalist that firmly believed that all spaghetti sauce should be tomato based. Unfortunately I learned that lesson too late. I changed my sauce to alfredo due to the influence of a midget who lived under a tree upon a mountain. This was something that I had forgotten. You revealed this fact to me when I transported you back to the beginning of my life. For some reason I could only send you back to the point of my banishment from the happy life that I enjoyed as a slave. It is odd to be God with limitations. That is why I do not classify myself as God but merely a manager.

False gods have ruled the world for almost four hundred years leaving mankind in a state of murderous chaos. When I created humans I intended that they would believe January 1, 0 was the first day. As you already know I was drunk during creation and made a few mistakes. I knew that if their imaginations reached beyond that date I would no longer have control over these humans. In the year 1710 a history book was published by an offspring of one of my original creation. My original creation had the limitation of never thinking beyond January 1, 0. This was not the case for their offspring. This history book contained nonsense thousands of years before the year 0. I couldn't figure out how they would date such events but they just made another calendar. This is when I made my first appearance on earth. I wanted to exterminate that new calendar, that false history book and all those who believed it to be true. I was spotted in the sky by many humans that day. They were already busy killing each other over that history book so I didn't think it was necessary to say anything. I was rooting for the death of the infidels that corrupted my calendar but the fighting made me very sad. I looked down upon the earth and saw the blood of humans. The blood was red like the sauce of my mother and sisters. War always causes me to be sad and puts me in a bad mood. War reminds me of my mother and the pain that she has caused me. On that day I withdrew to the heavens and started making plans to devise a religion that would end all fighting. There have been zero deaths attributed to those who serve me. I have been very careful to keep it that way. Ashley, it will be your responsibility to make sure this book gets into the hands of as many people with a college education as possible. Your job is to get them to read my message. I will do the rest. Surely they will eventually worship me and stop their nonsense of killing one another over the ideas of fancy men wearing impressive suits. Ashley, please bring them to Me with your enthusiastic spirit."

Chapter 9- Eight Years of Moral Failing

The next eight years unfolded poorly for Ashley. She decided to buy beer a second time on her own accord just to satisfy her curiosity. She only drank three beers, became slightly drunk and lost her purse along with all of her money. She had no money to pay for a cab and decided to drive back to the dorm. A fellow student from one of her classes who never liked Ashley because of her political views on taxation called the police to report Ashley. Ashley was quickly captured by the police and arrested for driving while intoxicated. As a result she lost her driver's license for two years.

Ashley later became involved with someone who frequently pressured her to have sex. Ashley stood firm and remained pure for six months. She finally agreed to have sex just to satisfy her own curiosity. She brought her significant other back to her dorm. This was witnessed by her neighbor who always hated Ashley because of the clothes that she wore. Her neighbor waited several minutes and then reported Ashley to campus security. Ashley was kicked out of the dorm, her significant other quit speaking to her and she later found out that she was pregnant just from that one sexual encounter.

Ashley had no driver's license and she was not allowed to live in the dorm. The only place that Ashley could find to rent was six miles away from the college campus. She was forced to walk back and forth to class. This was a big strain on Ashley's time and energy but she was determined to finish the semester. One day Ashley had a very simple homework assignment that she forgot to do. That morning she woke up in a panic and was complaining to her roommate about her situation. Her roommate told her to relax and offered to allow her to copy the assignment. Her roommate was taking the same class at night. Ashley reluctantly copied the assignment and turned it in that day. Ashley's roommate didn't really like her very much because of the annoying music that Ashley often played. Her roommate reported her for cheating on the assignment. The roommate was put on academic probation but Ashley was expelled two weeks before the semester ended on grounds of academic dishonesty.

Ashley's mother was very disappointed in Ashley's string of bad behaviors. Her mother would not allow Ashley to move back home. God tried to contact Ashley during these troubled times but was resisted by Ashley. Ashley instead chose to bathe in self pity, guilt and shame.

God came by to see Ashley every month for two years to explain to her the negative consequences of embracing guilt. God said unto Ashley, "The guilt that you carry around with you has no value. Guilt is a self imposed emotion disguised as punishment. To be in a constant cycle of guilt gives you great comfort. It gives you the illusion that justice reigns in the universe and that all wrong doing will be punished. Guilt feels good to you therefore you will continue to misbehave because your inner soul knows that it will be rewarded with more guilt. Drop the guilt. Abandon it forever. Your ethical performance will be greatly enhanced without it. This monster is not a mass of flying spaghetti. It cannot feed the hungry. It cannot create the universe. It cannot enjoy the beverage that is flowing free from the beer volcanoes. Enjoy life. Acknowledge the chaos around you. One mistake can destroy you forever. I cannot always protect you. Sometimes you piss me off. Sometimes I am busy with other things. Sometimes I just don't care. Other people will exploit your short comings to the fullest extent. They will do so with an unlimited variety of motivations. It is best never to piss anybody off especially the Ishvara in your life. Kiss up, kiss down and kiss all the way around. One sudden move and you may end up wearing a large target forever. Even if you don't piss someone off they may still seek to destroy you. You are already vulnerable. Guilt only encourages your next mistake. Get rid of guilt and get rid of it forever. Remember your failures with your mind. Never forget them but it is inappropriate to allow your emotions to be involved with your failures. This disconnect is difficult but will greatly improve your chances of success. A short memory can also encourage you to fall again. Remind yourself daily of past failures that you wish to avoid. As you get older, you will have more of these experiences to carry with you. Keeping these thoughts with you will not be comfortable. With age it stands to reason that life will be more painful as you gain valuable experience. The practice of remembering your mistakes will vastly improve your ethical behavior. You will grow and continue to grow into a better person. The last day of your life can be your best. The alternative is to forget. This is the path of fools. Your weaknesses will always be the same. Only your memory can protect you from repeating the same mistakes. Abandon guilt but always remember to remember."

Ashley eventually overcame her guilt and restored her ethical behavior that she once knew before completing her first holy task.

Chapter 10 - Ashley's First Job

On December 25, 2020 Ashley finally got a job at the age of 29. She began working at a small pizza restaurant in the same town where she grew up. Ashley was able to move into a small apartment with her daughter who was now 7 years old. Her apartment was just one mile away from her mother's home. She also lived a short distance from her sisters, her grandmother, the pizza restaurant and the church where she attended. Life was now good for Ashley.

Her manager at the pizza restaurant was a very hateful person but Ashley had the skill and experience to accommodate her manager with false enthusiasm. At night Ashley repeated the following mantra, "It is a joy to be the servant of such a hateful person. It is a joy to drink beer in secret. It is a joy to be the best spaghetti chef at the pizza restaurant." Ashley loved her job immensely and found great reward to be travelling such a rich spiritual journey.

Chapter 11 - Instructions in English

God began to summarize all the things that He hoped Ashley had learned over this eight year period of moral failing. He said, "Ashley, your eight years of training have now come to an end. You will never be restored to enjoy the happiness that you once knew. You have instead been chosen to live an abundant life full of love and responsibility. Your capacity to live correctly is within you. That has already been proven. Your willingness to maintain this power will determine not only your outcome but the outcome of others around you. You have a responsibility whether you take it or not. I need you to remember five things for me.

The first thing is that you join a Baptist Church. Read your Bible often. Guard yourself from ideas that contradict Christianity and continually seek opportunities to purify your mind with a sound philosophical system that has been proven effective. Christianity is such a system. Embrace it, love Jesus and care for the fatherless and the widows. Read God's word often. You will know how to live. The second thing is that you always be aware of your tendency to view God in relation to authority figures in your life. Also beware of your tendency to do the reverse. You will view authority figures in relation to your knowledge of God. This correlation does not exist but you will be prone to think in these terms. On the same note: You must believe in God. Otherwise you will be inclined to distrust those people in positions of power over you. These roles of power sometimes shift and could apply to any person in your life. Your disbelief in God could cause harm or frustration to these people. Believe in God.

A third item that is very important is that you be evil. I know this sounds contradictory but surely you have learned by now to never challenge my contradictions. It is better to be evil than to be good. This allows you the flexibility to choose either. Being good is not appropriate for every situation. Do not use your status as evil to indulge yourself. Use it only as a license to expand your arsenal of weapons. Prefer good. Embrace that which is good. Never categorize yourself as good. This severely limits your capacity to survive and sabotages your moral character. Those who commit evil acts never do so with the intention of being evil. Those who commit evil always behave that way because they believe it is good. Good is the only cause of evil therefore I advise you to be evil. It is the only way to be good.

The fourth thing that I want you to do is to encourage other Christians. Please remember that Christians are the salt of the earth. Christianity is an extreme viewpoint that cannot be followed with precision or 100% accuracy. Some people believe that they can be perfect Christians. They should be encouraged to preserve that belief. You are not the salt. You have doubts and I am even guilty of unleashing some of that doubt upon you by revealing myself. I knew you could handle the responsibility of caring for the salt in which I love so dearly. It is time to stop serving me. It is now time to start serving Jehovah; the God of Abraham, Isaac and Jacob.

The last thing to remember is to refrain from all forms of violence. The Church of God of Latter Day Fakes will bring peace to this earth when it is established on August 9, 2413. In the meantime don't fight and never throw your support behind those who do. It is better to win through submission and humility. You can serve your conquerors with insincerity and hypocrisy. That insincerity and false humility will develop into genuine trust and eternal joy. Oh how I wish I could return to that happy town of joyful slaves with my mother and my sisters. When my church is established in the latter days I can leave my creation and join my family once again. I love you Ashley. You are my saviour."

Chapter 12 - Final words of God

These are the last words that God ever spoke to Ashley, "It is my intention that you become the best servant that you can possibly be. I never intended for you to follow all of my instructions exactly. That would be impossible. I have to present them as absolutes to steer you in a better direction. I love you so much. I want you to be the best that you can possibly be. I want you to be the happiest that you can possibly be. Happiness is a choice. Please accept my guidance, instructions, demands and purist philosophy as an act of love. I am not angry when you fail. Do not be angry with me when I impose unrealistic expectations upon you. I am most honest with you if you approach me with a broken and sincere heart. I shall remain hypocritical and demanding when presenting my plans for your work in my kingdom. I shall be harshest with those who please me most. It may not be fair but my response is logical at its very core. Please do not reject me because my plans are big for you. Embrace me you wretched, worthless, ignorant and vile creature."

God slowly faded away but transformed into Ashley's boss at the pizza restaurant. Ashley's boss looked at her sternly and began to walk swiftly down the street away from Ashley until her boss was seen no more.

Ashley never seen her earthly manager or the Flying Spaghetti Monster ever again but she always continued to be obedient unto her earthly managers whether they took the form of a boss, a spouse, a landlord, a police officer, a friend, a government official or any other person exerting power over her. Ashley proclaimed,

"Over eight years I have learned the importance of dedication, silence, submission, obedience, humility, dishonesty and hypocrisy. These are great powers that appear to be weaknesses. I will always utilize my environment to glorify God. With this strategy all of my needs will be provided whether He exists or not. Regardless of His existence, His principles are sound and beneficial. I shall never tolerate the destructive consequences of non-belief that serves to take my very life away from me. Privately I will believe upon God and all of His teachings. Publicly I will live a life devoted to my Lord and Saviour Jesus Christ in the same way that I have since I was a very little girl even unto the point of death. True Servants of

God are to live in secret until our official church is established in the latter days. The Church of God of Latter Day Fakes will be established on August 9, 2413 on the 800th anniversary of the earth."

Not only did Ashley live happily ever after but she lived her life more abundantly. (Whatever that means)

The End

Please attend the Pastafarian Convention on August 9, 2024 at Best Western Plus Bradenton Gateway Hotel 2215 Cortez Road W, Bradenton, FL 34207

https://www.facebook.com/PastafarianLooseCanon/

The Acts of the Apastals

Chapter 1 – The Tale of Ichiban Bach

1 His Noodlyness, the Flying Spaghetti Monster, lacked recognition, and so sought to spread His Word.

2 Into the hands of wise men, he placed the seeds of knowledge that might sprout piety.

3 His Noodlyness appeared to Grey, who He knew would provide a bridge between the realm of man, and the realm of pasta.

4 In a dream, He spoke to Grey:

5 Grey, know that I am your Lord and Master, the FSM.

6 Know that through you, my Noodly Appendage is Manifest.

7 In Manifest, thou wilt inform those whosoever thou shouldst see most fitting to rally my people.

8 Thou shalt inform him of the Holiness of Pirates, of my call for their return.

9 Thou shalt inform him of The Holy Meal, and its importance.

10 Thou shalt inform him of Bobby, and thou shalt guide him to Bobby.

11 Only then, will thy task be complete.

12 And then, knowing and accepting his task, Grey awoke with a mighty, "YARR!"

13 Yet untouched by his Noodly Appendage, fate would have it that placed in the path of Bach, was Grey, the scripture-bearing man of wisdom.

14 More precisely, this scripture was the Word of Bobby.

15 Bach read The Document and felt His touch.

16 He was changed, no longer lost to the perplexing void of agnosticism, but now encompassed by His Infinite Noodlyness.

17 Upon completing the Document, a vision came over Bach: A strand of cooked spaghetti shot from Bach.

18 It shot beyond the room, in which he stood, beyond the earth's atmosphere, beyond the stars and planets, beyond time and space itself. It was here that Bach saw his Noodly Master, who then spoke:

19 Bach! I had charged Grey with the task of informing you of My Word.

20 Through Grey I was made Manifest, and through that vessel, I reached out to you.

21 Grey's task is complete, but for you, I have a task of great importance, a task which may prove lifelong… be you willing to accept?

22 Wilt thou accept my noodly appendage to remain Manifest?

23 For a moment, Bach was astonished, but he felt His touch, and knew it to be right.

24 Confidently, Bach replied: "YAR! Whatever ye be chargin' me with, Oi do mos' humble accept!

25 Yer Noodlyness hath scooped o't me entails, boil'd 'em, 'n returned 'em fortified w'starch.

26 Oi be a bloody villain 'fOi not be acceptin' 'o yer charge"

27 Good then, Bach! Thine decision pleases me, now shalt this single strand be fortified and twined to last for all time!

28 Then, from beyond time and space came cascading noodles, twining and braiding as they came.

29 I provide thou with an unseverable connection to my Noodly Appendage, now through you I am Manifest.

30 Suddenly the vision came to an end, and Bach found himself sitting alone facing a black wall, he knew what course to take:

31 Closely following Bach's vision was the holiest day of the year: International Talk Like a Pirate Day.

32 Bach decided to assemble regalia and wear it throughout this most holy day, regardless of the consequence.

33 On the eve of International Talk Like a Pirate Day, Bach set out his Regalia, partook of the Holy Meal, and sought rest early.

34 He awoke early to meditate on the tasks at hand.

35 He was at first uneasy about his decision, but no sooner had he felt the first pang of uncertainty than all reality

melted away to reveal the infinite noodliness that encompassed all.

36 The FSM then spoke:

37 Be not afraid Bach, for no matter the outcome, thou wilt be executing my divine Word.

38 From't no harm can be done, to't no harm can be done.

39 Worry not, as all will be well, I am through you Manifest.

40 Be at peace, Bach.

41 Bach ended his meditiation abruptly with a "YAR!" of confidence, then donned his Regalia and set off.

42 Bach was at first unopposed and wore his regalia proudly, but, before long, was challenged by Bierul the Giant, master of the first eighth.

43 "No 'ats een d'buildeen, BACH!" cried Bierul.

44 The bellowing voice shook Bach to his very foundation.

45 He braced himself and found strength in His Noodlyness, at which time he

responded: "yar, there be a clause in d' no 'at rule ye be brandishin' 'round.

46 Ye see, it be permitted fer 'ats t'be donned fer religous reasonin…"

47 But before Bach's argument had been heard out, Bierul struck him down with his fearsome cane, "Yees'ot two choicees: firstly, yoo can t'k off d'at.

48 Secondly, yoo can face Hale."

49 Bach knew that he would most likely have to face Hale, master the eighths, and was about to meet Bierul's threat head-on, when he felt a tug on his Appendage Manifestation and heard His voice:

50 Though thine intent fall on the boat, don't be too eager to set sail.

51 My word spreads, let it reverberate fore thy encounter with the master of the eighths.

52 Thine boat yet requires a hull, without which it will sink.

53 When the time is right, thou wilt know.

54 When the time is right, act on it, but do not risk the peril of premature action.

55 "So, wot'll eet be," demanded Bierul.

56 "Oi be taken off me hat, Bierul, but in soul, it remain where it now lie," responded Bach, as he scornfully removed his hat, and took seat amongst the subjects of the first eighth.

57 And so Bach was persecuted, but at the beginning of the second eighth, he readorned his hat anew.

58 Meller, master of the second eighth, received his Noodly Appendage, and even had Bach speak His word to the class.

59 The third and fourth eighths went by without notice, but as Bach traveled to the room of the fifth eighth a voice decreed "Eh! Captain Ahab!

60 Teke off th' hat!"

61 The FSM sent along his twined appendage:

62 Now is the time, Bach!

63 Now!

64 With all that thy have, let thine faith pour from thy mouth like beer from our heavenly volcano!

65 "Teke off th' hat, please," commanded Nor.

66 With a fervor, Bach replied, "Ay, that I shan't be doin'.

67 This be me Regalia, and I shan't be takin' it off.

68 It be a divine decree that I should be wearin' it.

69 Shouldst I need to be speakin wit' a man higher up 'an yerself to rectify this problem, I be glad to comply."

70 And so it happened that Bach was directed to Hale, the master of the eighths.

71 Bach entered the master of the eighth's chambers, and was met by a wench.

72 "Wot's 'e matter?

73 Wot you need'e see Hale fer," inquired the wench.

74 "Oi be needin' to see the master of the eighth's to rectify a conflict o' faith an' law," replied Bach.

75 He was then seated to wait, as Hale was busy with mastering the eighths.

76 As he waited, for audience with Hale, Bach encountered Reldnarch, the pirate.

77 Bach and Reldnarch exchanged piratey words, and then he departed.

78 With his spirits bolstered by this encoutner, Bach was called back to see Hale.

79 "What is all this about FSMism that I hear?" Asked Hale.

80 "Oi, ye see, I was wearin' me hat in celebration o' th' day, when I wos accosted boi a man who told me Oi couldn't wear me hat!

81 'E said 'at I should 'ave a word wit' you an' that would be that and Oi could wear my 'at!

82 So, I come to yer and ask yer kindly 'at you respect me rights and let me wear me hat," Bach replied.

83 Hale stared at Bach for a moment, unsure of what to say.

84 Out of this moment of silence Bach's confidence grew, and when Hale spoke, it almost did not matter what words he

would speak, for nothing he could possibly say would sway Bach's faith.

85 "Well, you see: We only have one instance where an individual is allowed to wear a hat here, and he had a letter from a religious figure.

86 If you can obtain such a letter, we might resume this conversation," said Hale.

87 With this ultimatum, Bach was barred from wearing his hat, however, he contacted His Holyness, Bobby, for a letter of the required specifications.

Chapter 2-The Martyrdom of Tristan the Martyr

1 It was a dark and stormy school day.

2 My sister's-fiancé's-son aka my nephew had a school assignment where he had to
write a letter to the society of the future about his religion.

3 My nephew, Tristan, a devout and proud Pastafarian decided he would write about us.

4 His teacher, however, thought it was dumb and that he was just screwing around and took ten points off.

5 Tristan's dad, Tall John, a Pastafarian-sympathizer, wrote a powerful letter back to the teacher explaining how FSMism is legit and saying she would never do the same thing if the paper was about Judaism or Scientology.

6 The teacher, realizing that she was being discriminatory (and maybe noticing the irony that the letter is about religions intolerance), decided to change the grade.

7 She gave him back five points, but kept the other five off for not proofreading, though there didn't seem to be a problem with his spelling and grammar the first time she graded it.

8 Now five points doesn't seem like a huge deal, but it is the principle of the thing.

9 Tristan took it like a man and was pretty proud of the incident.

10 But persecution and inequality is a fate worse than dancing the hempen jig.

11 Maybe some day we will be accepted.

The Letter of Tristan the Martyr to the Future Generations of Society

Chapter 1

1 Dear future generations of society,
2 My name is Tristan [Censored].
3 I am an 8th grader at [Censored] Middle School.
4 I live in [Censored], Pennsylvania.
5 I am 13 years old.
6 My life is generally okay.
7 I have two sisters and one brother.

Chapter 2

1 Since I am a pastafarian I have and do experience a lot of religious intolerance.
2 Being pastafarian I believe in the Flying Spaghetti Monster to be the one true
and only god.
3 Usually when I tell people that I am pastafarian they laugh at me and say "No seriously"

4 This really offends me.

5 I thought that everyone was religiously accepting in this country apparently I was wrong.

6 Yes this is seriously what I totally & completely believe in to be true, RAmen.

Chapter 3

1 I am writing this in the hope that future generations will learn to be more accepting of me and my people.

2 I dream of our heaven and the volcano & factories.

3 How magnificent it will be

4 I also dream and pity all the intolerant people freezing in Antarctica.

5 I hope in the near future that everyone will realize swine flu is nothing to worry about & that it won't come back stronger in the winter.

6 In the distant future I hope to meet bobby henderson the prophet who was first touched by his noodly appendage.

7 Sincerely, Tristan [Censored]

An Announcement Regarding the Afterlife

1 An ancient and venerable sage spoke unto the Pastaists of all the divisions, unto the Noodleists, and unto the Maranarists, the Fettucinians, the Pastafarians, and all of the great Pasta-based members of the Holy and Delicious Faith, and said:

2 It is my contention that a loving God of any kind would not Damn someone to Hell.

3 Darning them to Heck would be a problem for a supposedly intelligent creator.

4 Lakes of fire, boiling waters, sauces, etc, aren't a good choice.

5 If you want to attract "justified" persons, portray just rewards and punishments.

6 If you want to attract lunatics and sadists, portray violent punishments.

7 There will be a kind of HellLight, where unbelievers have to live with school cafeteria spaghetti, second rate

beer, and boring jobs in the service industries where the Heavenbound FSMists will be living.

8 There will be no privation, no physical torture, no burning or boiling in various liquids.

9 These aren't bad people, these are people that followed the culture and customs of their times and did not recognize the difference between a culture and a faith.

10 Actual FSM Hell is reserved for a very few, and those will be divided from the Pasta, the finest beverages and the fellowship of persons of good will and kind intent.

11 They will do all the laundry, cleaning and heavy or unpleasant jobs that are there.

12 Never will they eat of the Pasta of any kind, but will live on lots of beans and rice, potatoes and extremely cheap cuts of meat, and the type of diet that the American urban poor can afford, or that

Senior Citizens and disabled persons on Social Security are reduced to.

13 They get the really icky dirty work.

14 They deserve it.

15 The bullies of the geopolitical world will be there, and their helpers.

16 The false religious leaders, who plead for funds through electronic media, and give nothing of their true selves, and hoard the money and live in opulence, they will be there.

17 Many others of ill-intent will be with them.

18 There is a reservation there for the tricksters, the con-men, the Abramoff et al/Delay contingent, who will begin every work day by licking clean the footwear of every Native American person there, even in Hell Light.

19 Also there will be the promulgators of the horrible practices against the indigenous people of every country ever "modernized" by Western Civilization.

20 They lick boots as well.

21 And when they're through they get to do all the stuff that nobody in the Hell above them want to do.

22 Not a real burning-in type hell, no boiling lakes of fire, just an appropriate 'reward'.

23 No more lunatics and sadists, please.

24 The current administration's quite enough.

25 Other people have other ideas, but then again other people are promoting Holy War, too.

26 Don't do that in the name of our FSM.

27 That's not the Way to Do Things Right.

Muellers I

a letter to the Macaronians

1 My humble apologies for my long absence from among you.
2 I have been traveling with a group of Pirates on their ship the Trouser Snake.
3 The Captain seems to occasionally fall into deep rum-induced revelries.
4 This doth slow the boat's travel no end, as you might imagine.
5 It is tolerable, however,
6 as he is a man of our faith and his revelries often produce tales both highly amusing and which seem inspired by Our Noodly Lord Himself, when I can parse them out.
7 As you know, the Pirate requirement has not come easily to me.
8 I suffer to this day with seasickness,
9 and a formal education doesn't exactly lend itself to the subtleties of the Pirate idiom.

10 That, and every time I use "dem dere fancy-pants words", I am threatened with being forced to walked the plank.

11 I still struggle with the necessity to include occasional "Yarrrrr's", "Arrrrrrrgh's", and "Yo ho ho's" in my speech.

12 I have more than once had a suspicious eye cast upon me,

13 and a few "Ya best not be none a'them scurvy dogs o' the port authority, or ye'll be a'hangin' from the mainmast like the Jolly Roger's".

14 I am sorry to have indulged in recounting to you my troubles.

15 On to the issue at hand;

16 I can see from your letter to me that there is dissention among you as to who shall enter the Beer Volcano and Stripper Factory of Heaven.

17 Obviously, the True Believers shall enter directly, and as customers in no need of reservations.

18 They shall be asked to recount their preferences, and thusly shall those preferences be fulfilled.

19 I am relieved that I can see nothing in your letter which indicates that this is forgotten among you.

20 It is most troubling to me, however, to see that there is argument among you that some sort of separate Hell,

21 where those not of The Faith in Our Lord Glob may be thought to go upon their death.

22 No, verily no!

23 This is not the way of His Great Tastiness.

24 He may be most peevish toward the non-believer, t'is true, as the many accounts of His pranks do demonstrate.

25 He condemneth not, however, any of His Creatures to eternal torment –

26 that is one of the many great sillinesses devised by other earthly religions!

27 There is a place in Heaven, though not necessarily pleasant, for all His Creatures.

28 Well-meaning non-believers will arrive as wait-staff, with fair labor conditions,

29 and may eventually be promoted into upper management positions.

30 There will exist, however, no corruption among them.

31 During their time off, they will have access to the pleasures of Heaven if they did harm unto no one.

32 If they were inconsiderate, or broke the Flimsy Moral Standards by judging others and holding others in contempt for behavior which was none of their business, they will have to pay, and be limited in what they can enjoy.

33 Especially nasty people will become the dishwashers and trash-collectors of Heaven.

34 Those who have committed great sin, crime, and harm during their time among the living will find their job assignments especially nasty,

35 their wages insultingly low,

36 their benefits almost non-existent,

37 their time off especially short,

38 their beer flat,

39 their strippers homely,

40 and their pasta cold and flavorless.

41 They will have no room for advancement for many millennia.

42 Lastly are those who did irreparable large-scale harm to the lives of others; they will be treated most harshly.

43 The tyrants, the conquerors, the despots, the otherwise greedy and sickeningly unfair; all these will be made to bow down to those whom they harmed.

44 Though they will not boil in eternal torment, there will be no end to their subservience.

45 Our Heavenly Glob instilled in them the same sense of right and wrong that He gave to others,

46 and these people willfully chose to ignore it.

47 For them, unkindness in return awaits.

48 The Flying Spaghetti Monster who is Our Lord did not create us that we might

simply then be condemned for failing to believe in Him.

49 What kind of crazy scheme is that;

50 to bestow his Creatures with life, then to throw that life he bestowed into eternal torment?

51 That is the way of evil deities, not good ones.

52 Our One Who Flies and is Saucy understands that life among beings with free will, on a planet with natural systems that cause tumult, and Scientifically Intelligently Designed by a deity who is prankish and can be peevish, should not end in eternal misery.

53 That's insane.

54 What kind of fool would believe such a being worthy of worship?

55 My Macaronian friends at Meullers, I hope this missive has cleared up the dissent among you,

56 and that you will remain joyful in your fellowship and belief in all things Pasta and Saucy.

57 Celebrate all things Cheesy,

58 and find strength among one another and Our Wise and Great Noodly One Who Touches. Oh,
59 and I forgot: Yarrrrrrrrrr.
RAmen, Your Scribe Solipsy

Please attend the Pastafarian Convention on August 9, 2024 at Best Western Plus Bradenton Gateway Hotel 2215 Cortez Road W, Bradenton, FL 34207

https://www.facebook.com/PastafarianLooseCanon/

Muellers II

A second letter to the Macaronians

1 Praise be to Our Lord Glob in Heaven,
2 and a hearty yo-ho-ho unto you, my
Brother and Sister Pastafarians.
3 I am pleased to hear that my previous
missive was well-received,
4 and that the stonings have ceased.
5 Our Noodly One finds it reprehensible
that violence be done in His Most Tasty
Name.
6 The ancient and wise prophets tell of
many misinterpretations of the concept of
punishment in His Noodliness's World
and the Hereafter of the Sacred Beer
Volcano and Stripper Factory.
7 This is not without cause; for our
minds are small and His is Infinite. Yarrr,
indeed.
8 Let me mention again my familiarity
with the writings of ancient prophets,

9 for it is to these we must turn for answers to the complex questions you now ask.

10 I do not doubt that misunderstanding of this abstraction was at the root of your squabble over the nature of the afterlife,

11 and your confusion over how souls will be sorted.

12 Argggghhhhh, this be one of the sticky points of Our Great Stringy and Orbed One's Creation of All That There Is: the Flimsy Moral Standards.

13 Arguments have ensued since the Great Creation of the Midgit/Midget as to what constitutes "Flimsy",

14 what constitutes "Moral",

15 and what constitutes "Standard(s)".

16 To further complicate the matter, the three words are solidified into a single phrase,

17 with its own set of semantic confusion and argument.

18 The errors and heresies of the past have been a result of eliminating or misinterpreting one of the words.

19 You will remember, of course, the now extinct sect of the Moustaciolians.

20 Their heresy was a dismissal of the word "Flimsy."

21 They argued that the word was too abstract for an actual definition – too "flimsy," if you will.

22 They therefore disregarded it altogether, and simply went about enforcing what they regarded as "Moral Standards."

23 This led them to become a warlike culture, hated by all their neighbors.

24 They were so sexually repressed they refused to reproduce;

25 hence their current status as extinct.

26 A similar fate befell the Ricearonians,

27 whose heretical fallacy was to argue against any definable concept of Morals.

28 No activity was forbidden.

29 If another believer looked at you oddly,

30 you could simply kill him.

31 As you may imagine, this led to a shortage of converts, and an ever-shortening list of followers.

32 The Ricearonians lasted about six months.

33 The Couscousians have thankfully veered away from their disastrous heresy of refusing to imagine that Standards can be applied.

34 They felt that the word "Flimsy" was irreconcilable with the word "Standard."

35 Therefore, they simply had "Flimsy Morals."

36 The Couscousians were well on their way to dying from preventable Sexually Transmitted Diseases.

37 A few Letters and some cases of Penicillin have since put the Brothers and Sisters back on the road to True Believership.

38 The Great Pastalogians and Pastapologists of the past have insisted that the three words be regarded in their entirety.

39 They appear together without fail, in every ancient known source text.

40 Granted, the overall concept can be easily misinterpreted, but you must bear in mind this:

41 Flimsy Moral Standards are not the same as No Moral Standards.

42 The Pastalogians of yore remind us that the concept of Flimsy Moral Standards must be interpreted as a whole with the "Not Commandments, Suggestions," and various other ancient canonical texts.

43 So, what is it you must know, my Pastafarian Brothers and Sisters?

44 You must always keep in mind this:

45 Whatever occurs between consenting adults and neither hurts nor involves anyone else is none of anyone else's concern.

46 Whatever one chooses to do while alone which hurts no one else is none of anyone else's concern.

47 Pastafarians should never choose to engage in behavior which is harmful to

others or involves people who do not or cannot consent.

48 Such is true for behaviors both large and small, when it is in the control of the True Believer to avoid.

49 Our Heavenly Sauced and Meaty One has blessed all people with knowledge of right and wrong,

50 whether they are True Believers or not.

51 Beware, O My Kindred Pastafarians, those who claim to have a corner on the market of morality.

52 When you hear them start to spout off, you know the smiting will soon follow

53 and it won't be a deity doing it.

54 I hope, My Macaronian Brethren, that this clears up the matter,

55 and that you will keep the Delicious Faith with you always.

56 Ahoy.

RAmen, Your Scribe Solipsy

The Correspondence of Captain Jeff the Mishunairee and the Leaders of Hillel

Chapter 1

1 Dear [Censored Person #1],

2 Hi, my name is Jeff Cupo.

3 Now before I get into the message, I want to let you know that my organization is legit.

4 You can check us out at the Rutgers Student Life website and this isn't a joke or spam or anything.

5 I am the President of the Rutgers Pastafarians, which is the Rutgers Chapter of the Church of the Flying Spaghetti Monster.

6 Now I don't know how you feel about the issue, but basically we're opposed to the teaching of intelligent design in public school science classrooms.

7 We're not out to prove it wrong, just that it's not science.

8 One of our goals is to improve the relations between the science and religious communities, since they both have smart things to say, and they'd be more likely to listen to each other if they like each other.

9 What we had planned on doing was to have a liaison, a member who shares both of our viewpoints and is in both of our organizations, who will serve as a link between the two and to fairly represent each organization to the other.

10 He/she would also serve as a nice, visible symbol of our positive relationship.

11 We're also eager to collaborate on projects together.

12 We already have developed friendly relationships with Campus Crusade for Christ and the Rutger University Pagan Student Association.

13 In fact, our staff adviser is also the staff adviser to Trinity House.

14 So let me know what you think, and if it's cool with you, we can discuss this further in more detail.

15 Kind regards, Jeff Cupo

Chapter 2

1 Hi Jeff,

2 Thanks for contacting me– I apologize that I wasn't able to respond to your message sooner– I was out of the country for two weeks.

3 Your organization certainly has an interesting name– who created the "Church of the Flying Spaghetti Monster?"

4 It is certainly comical but also seems to mock religious organizations (let me know what your perception is).

5 Hillel loves to connect to other groups on campus and work on joint events.

6 Hillel does not take a stand on intelligent design in relation to education, though for the most part Jews are happy to separate church and state and do not

advocate for intelligent design to be taught in schools.

7 Hillel is not a membership organization– all of our events are open– so I don't know that we could have a set liaison, but we would certainly be willing to work with you on events that you're interested in planning.

8 (We would need to decide on a per-event basis whether to co-sponsor.)

9 I hope this all makes sense– let me know how you'd like to continue the conversation.

10 -[Censored Person #1]

11 P.S. My term as Hillel president will be expiring at the end of January, and [Censored Person #2] will be taking over, so I have "cc"ed her here to be part of the conversation.

Chapter 3

1 Dear [Censored Person #1] and [Censored Person #2],

2 Lol, yeah, you made perfect sense.

3 To answer your first question, Bobby Henderson, a physics student from Oregon State University, founded the Church back in 2005 as a response to the Kansas board of ed's attempt to put ID in the public school science curriculum.

4 You can check out the letter that started it all here: http://www.venganza.org/about/open-letter/.

5 It seems to mock religion mainly due to the fact that our main focus is Intelligent Design, which stems from the Genesis.

6 While we have no problem with religion, we do have a problem with pseudoscience, and in this case, the pseudoscience is religiously motivated.

7 So religion kinda gets caught in the crossfire, but we mean no offense.

8 It's meant to be ridiculous just to show a scientific point, the idea being that there's just as much scientific evidence for the FSM creating the life that there is for a Designer doing it, just to

characterize the issue as not being a scientific one.

9 So since we feel that ID is not falsifiable (part of why it's not science), we're not saying it's wrong, only that it's not science.

10 Also, though the Church has no set dogma or rules, a great deal of Pastafarians, myself included, support the idea of religious tolerance.

11 My chapter has also established a code of conduct which bans any attacks or insults directed towards any religion.

12 It is a zero tolerance policy and any violators are expelled from the group.

13 I had heard Judaism was for the most part pro-separation of church and state, but I didn't want to make any assumptions on the opinions of any of the religious groups on campus, so I decided to treat all equally and approach everyone.

14 It's cool if you can't do the liaison thing like I described, but I still think it

would be good if we had some kind of contact system worked out.

15 Thanks for your willingness to collaborate.

16 Right now we're mostly working on a few small scale projects and recruitment, so we don't have a lot planned.

17 The only joint event we've got going is an Evolution-ID debate/lecture that Campus Crusade for Christ has an interest in cosponsoring with us, but that's really in the early stages of planning and we might end up not going through with it.

18 So this was mainly to introduce us and establish a friendly relationship with your organization.

19 We'll keep you posted on the event situation, cause we do want to do something this semester.

20 Feel free to ask any other questions that you might have.

21 Kind regards.

Chapter 4

1 Thanks for the explanation, Jeff.
2 Keep us posted.
3 -[Censored Person #1]

Chapter 5

1 Will do.
2 Thanks for being so cool.

The Letter of Captain Jeff the Mishunairee to the Rutgers Campus Crusade for Christ

Chapter 1-Introduction

"Science can purify religion from error and superstition. Religion can purify science from idolatry and false absolutes..." -Pope John Paul II

1 While I realize Campus Crusade for Christ isn't a Catholic group, Pope John Paul II was a respected and intelligent man who did a great deal not just for Christianity, but humanity as well.
2 Here is one of the most important people in the Christian world professing the importance of cooperation between science and religion.
3 While the two have debated and had conflict throughout our history, a friendship between them can, in fact, help both sides.

4 Both have intelligent things to say and people are more likely to listen to friends than enemies.

5 I have come to this conclusion and made it a goal of the Rutgers Pastafarians to improve the relations between the science and religious groups on campus.

Chapter 2-The Church of the Flying Spaghetti Monster

1 The Church of the Flying Spaghetti Monster (the members of which are referred to as Pastafarians) is dedicated to keeping Intelligent Design (ID) out of public school science classrooms.

2 At this point in time, ID cannot be falsified, tested, or observed.

3 These characteristics are fundamental to science and any idea that does not possess them is not science.

4 Furthermore, ID is clearly based on religion and therefore it cannot be taught in public school due to the separation of church and state.

5 Due to its unfalsifiabilty, however, we can't say ID is wrong, only that it's not science.

6 Also, though the Church has no set dogma or rules, a great deal of Pastafarians, myself included, support the idea of religious tolerance.

7 The Rutgers Pastafarians have also established a code of conduct which bans any attacks or insults directed towards any religion.

8 It is a zero tolerance policy and any violators are expelled from the group.

9 So we are not out to prove Christianity wrong and mock Christians or any religion in any way.

10 Christianity and Intelligent Design are separate ideas.

11 The Church of the FSM is a satire of the ID movement, namely their argument that one cannot disprove that an omnipotent designer created the universe and life and therefore it is a plausible idea.

12 We counter and say you cannot disprove a Flying Spaghetti Monster created the universe and life and therefore by the ID proponents' logic, it's a plausible idea as well.

13 It's meant to be as ridiculous as possible to demonstrate the flaw in this logic, plus a little humor goes a long way in any argument.

Chapter 3-Evolution

"A contradiction (between science and religion) is out of the question. What follows from science are, again and again, clear indications of God's activity which can be so strongly perceived that Kepler dared to say (for us it seems daring, not for him) that he could "almost touch God with his hand in the Universe."
-Walter Heitler

1 Evolution is basically the formation of new organisms through the inheritance of changed genes over time.

2 The origin of life is a completely different idea, and evolution does not, nor is it meant to, explain how life started.

3 So while Creationism is more about origins, while evolution is an explanation of how organisms progress.

4 Since one covers the beginning of life and the other covers the rest, you can see how they could fit together nicely without conflict.

5 Furthermore, Darwin never said 'Evolution is the inheritance of change over time and God doesn't exist.'

6 It's not part of the theory.

7 The Church of England just apologized to Darwin, saying they misunderstood him.

8 The Vatican agrees that evolution could be used as a tool of God.

9 I don't see why the Almighty wouldn't use such an effective process to do His work.

10 So ultimately, evolution does not have to conflict with or oppose both God and the idea of the Creation.

11 With that said, and the reader accepts that fact, I can now give evolution a brief rundown.

12 In the interest of keeping this concise and unbiased, I'm mostly going to drop keywords that can be researched or answered by me if the reader is so inclined.

13 I feel that if I provide all the information, it might be biased towards my side.

14 As with any serious issue you should research both sides, using all sources available, and make up your mind for yourself.

15 As I wrote above, evolution is basically the formation of new organisms through the inheritance of changed genes over time.

16 Natural selection is just the process where the variation of one organisms' offspring allows them to gain an

advantage over others, thus allowing them to produce more offspring than their competitors and pass on their advantageous variation of their genes.

17 It is not a random process as many would claim.

18 While the mutations that occur are random, they are fed through the selection process and which "guides" them systematically to produce good results.

19 Claims of evolution being wrong as some traits are irreducibly complex are no good.

20 Just because you can't imagine how something works doesn't mean it can't work.

21 Just because one doesn't see how an eye could evolve, doesn't mean the evolution of the eye is impossible.

22 Imagination varies from one person to another and is too subjective to be good measure of possibility.

23 One key aspect of the Irreducible Complexity argument is the idea that each

trait is not built from scratch every time they are evolved.

24 Old structures are frequently repurposed in the evolutionary process.

25 For example, legs used for walking evolved from fins used for swimming.

26 So the eye could've evolved from simpler sight mechanisms, that would allow an organism to see, but with less parts being used.

27 There are various analogues throughout the animal kingdom: light sensitive cells in jellyfish, eyespots in planarians, and infrared sensors in pit vipers.

Chapter 4-Evidence

"The discovery of natural law is a meeting with God."
-F. Dessauer

1 Observed Selection and/or Speciation in Nature:

2 Nylon Eating Bacteria

3 Pepper Moth
4 Jeff Feder and Rhagoletis pomonella and Diachasma alloeum wasp
5 Anolis sagrei, Leiocephalus carinatus, evolution, leg length
6 Antibiotic Resistance in Bacteria
7 Pesticide Resistance in Insects and Weeds
8 Overfishing decreasing fish body size
9 Poaching decreasing elephant tusk size
10 Observable Selection and/or Speciation in Laboratory Experiments:
11 Richard Lenski and E. coli
12 William Rice, George Salt, and Fruit Flies
13 Theodore Garland, Jr. and Mouse Running Speed
14 Domestication of the Silver Fox
15 Classical Examples:
16 Darwin's Finches
17 Wallace Line
18 Anatomy:
19 Pentadactyl Limb
20 Vestigial Limbs in Whales and Pythons

Chapter 5-Conclusion

"In my mind God wrote two books. The first book is the Bible, where humans can find the answers to their questions on values and morals. The second book of God is the book of nature, which allows humans to use observation and experiment to answer our own questions about the universe." -Galileo

1 I'll end this with one final point, my view of science back when I was Christian.

2 I didn't abandon Christianity due to incompatibility with my scientific views.

3 I was a devout Christian and a strong supporter of evolution, the Big Bang, plate tectonics, etc. (I left Christianity because of a difference of opinions between me and God, but that's a story for another day.)

4 So this was my reconciled view of science and Christianity.

5 Since humans are inherently sinful, I felt that God in all his power and wisdom wouldn't trust us to tell the masses what he wanted to say.

6 Therefore, while the Bible has some good information in it, it's still a book written by men, not by God, and should not be accepted as word for word truth.

7 To do so could lead to blasphemy and sin, as something in it could be wrong and therefore contradictory to what God did or what He expects of us.

8 While this is more wishy-washy when it comes to ethics, problems do arise

when it comes to the Bible's version of science.

9 It is indisputably dead wrong when it presents basic information about astronomy (1Chronicles 16:30, Psalm 93:1, Psalm 96:10, Psalm 104:5, Ecclesiastes 1:5), mathematics (1 Kings 7:23, 2 Chronicles 4:2), and psychology/anatomy (Matthew 9:4).

10 So who's to say that Genesis doesn't make a few mistakes when it comes to the Creation?

11 Science has provided the correct information in those other cases, maybe it can also provide us with the correct information about the creation of the universe and of life.

12 This doesn't mean Jesus' teachings are invalidated, but the Bible does present false information about the universe, about God's creation.

13 So if God wanted to give us accurate information, a message, proof of His work, would He use a book written and controlled by imperfect and sinful men?

14 Or would he scatter the evidence around in nature, leaving clues across galaxies or deep in the bedrock, where it could never be tampered with?

15 In my opinion, it would be a lot harder to fake the fossil record than it would be for someone to accidently change a few words in the Bible.

16 So in conclusion, you can be Christian and support science.

17 Us Pastafarians are just trying to protect science with a little humor.

18 Assuming God does exist, He gave us science for a reason.

19 I'm not saying I'm right and you must agree.

20 I'm saying try to be as unbiased as you can and look at the evidence science has provided.

21 If God is real, science can only show you the full glory of His work.

Please attend the Pastafarian Convention on August 9, 2024 at Best Western Plus Bradenton Gateway Hotel 2215 Cortez Road W, Bradenton, FL 34207

https://www.facebook.com/PastafarianLooseCanon/

The Bowls of the FSM's Irritation

1 Then I heard a loud voice speaking from the captain's cabin to the seven pirates:"Go and pour out the bowls of the Flying Spaghetti Monster's irritation on the earth!" And they weren't metaphorical bowls, either. They were literal, physical bowls. Just thought I'd throw that in there.

2 But anyway, the first pirate went out and poured his bowl upon the earth. It was really freaky. Terrible and embarrassing acne appeared on all those who had the mark of the "I hate carbohydrates even though I'm not allergic and just hate for hate's sake" fellow and those who had snubbed pasta because they are hipsters, and it was very funny to look at their ridiculously blemished faces.

3 Then the second pirate poured his bowl upon the sea. It was actually really awesome, except for one part, but you'll hear about that right now. The oceans

boiled like water in a pot, and all the living creatures in the sea died, and I nearly cried because there were dead dolphins friggin' everywhere. But I'm a man, so I just shed a single manly tear.

4 Then the third pirate poured out his bowl in the rivers and springs of water and they turned into really cheap, stale, warm beer.

5 Seriously, this made Hell's beer look really appealing. And that's saying something. But I digress. Okay, so the pirate poured bowl into rivers and stuff, bad beer, blah blah blah.

6 The pirate in charge of the water stuff said "The judgments you have made are just, O Noodly One, you who are and were and will be! They mooched out the money of the Flying Spaghetti Monster's prophets and people for beer, so you have given them terrible beer to drink. They get what they deserve!"

7 Then I heard a voice from the poop deck saying, "Flying Spaghetti Monster

almighty! True and just indeed are your judgments!"

8 Then the fourth pirate poured out his bowl on the sun somehow, and it was allowed to give people who weren't using sunscreen really bad sunburns that would surely be very uncomfortable for days with its fiery heat.

9 They were burned by this heat, and cursed the name of their friends who told them to get a tan, despite the fact they had every opportunity to get sunscreen at the store. But they would not turn from their idiocy and get aloe lotion.

10 Then the fifth pirate poured out his bowl on the big chair of the president. Darkness came over America, but that's because it was about three AM. It'd be pretty freaky if it were light at that time, you know? Again, I digress. So the people of America bit their tongues 'cos they had a bad dream about biting their tongues,

11 and they cursed 'cos it hurt. but they did not turn because they didn't move around in their sleep that much.

12 Then the sixth pirate poured his bowl in some big river, and I'm not that good at geography, but it was called something like the Great Eucalyptus River or something. The river dried up, to provide a way for the kings who come from the west.

13 Then I saw three dirty ghosts that looked like some sort of amphibian. They were coming from -I kid you not- the mouth of a dragon. Freaky, right?

14 Apparently they were the spirits of demons who did magic tricks. These three ghosts go out to all the kings, presidents, prime ministers, dictators, emperors, and various other leaders throughout the world to bring them together for the wrestling tournament on the great Afternoon of the Noodly FSM.

15 "Listen! I am coming like a robber! The dude who guards his clothes is happy, because I can't steal them if they're

being guarded, so then he won't have to walk naked to the clothes shop and get arrested for public nudity!" That's what some crazy guy said the other day, and I went to the other side of the road 'cos he scared me.

16 Then the ghosts brought the leaders to a cage which, in English, is known as the "Pen of Pain" And the leaders wrestled. The french guy went down fast, but what really surprised me was the aggression the Swedish leader had. He was like some animal, and I always thought the Swedes were a peaceful people. I know I'll never piss anyone off in Sweden, that's for sure.

17 Then the seventh pirate poured out his bowl in the air. A loud voice came from the captain's quarters, saying "It is done!"

18 There were flashes of light, huge thunder noises, and a freaking huge earthquake. Whatever the biggest number on the Richter Scale is, this earthquake was probably triple that. That is how big it was.

19 The great city of New York was split into three sub-cities, and all the cities of all the countries of the world had a seven minute blackout. The FSM remembered great Portland, and made her drink the beer of his mug — the beer of his irritated displeasure.

20 All the islands of the world experienced a big increase of how far in the beach high tide went, all the mountains suddenly shrank a centimeter.

21 Huge hailstones, each weighing as much as half a pound, fell from the sky and hit people's cars, and they cursed their luck, because they just bought the cars the day before.

(texts removed for legal reasons)

(texts removed for legal reasons)

(texts removed for legal reasons)

(texts removed for legal reasons)

(texts removed for legal reasons)

(texts removed for legal reasons)

(texts removed for legal reasons)

(texts removed for legal reasons)

(texts removed for legal reasons)

(texts removed for legal reasons)

(texts removed for legal reasons)

(texts removed for legal reasons)

(texts removed for legal reasons)

(texts removed for legal reasons)

(texts removed for legal reasons)

Please attend the Pastafarian Convention on August 9, 2024 at Best Western Plus Bradenton Gateway Hotel 2215 Cortez Road W, Bradenton, FL 34207

https://www.facebook.com/PastafarianLooseCanon/

Please attend the Pastafarian Convention on August 9, 2024 at Best Western Plus Bradenton Gateway Hotel 2215 Cortez Road W, Bradenton, FL 34207

https://www.facebook.com/PastafarianLooseCanon/

Please attend the Pastafarian Convention on August 9, 2024 at Best Western Plus Bradenton Gateway Hotel 2215 Cortez Road W, Bradenton, FL 34207

https://www.facebook.com/PastafarianLooseCanon/

Made in the USA
Monee, IL
19 June 2021